THE WISDOM OF BIG BIRD

(and the Dark Genius of Oscar the Grouch)

VILLARD / NEW YORK

THE WISDOM OF BIG BIRD

(and the Dark Genius of Oscar the Grouch)

LESSONS FROM A LIFE IN FEATHERS

CAROLL SPINNEY

with J milligan

ILLUSTRATIONS BY CAROLL SPINNEY

Copyright © 2003 by Caroll Spinney and Jason Milligan

All rights reserved under International and Pan-American
Copyright Conventions. Published in the United States by Villard Books,
an imprint of The Random House Ballantine Publishing Group, a division
of Random House, Inc., New York, and simultaneously in Canada
by Random House of Canada Limited, Toronto.

Villard Books and "V" Circled Design are registered
trademarks of Random House, Inc.

Library of Congress Cataloging-in-Publication Data
Spinney, Caroll
The wisdom of Big Bird (and the dark genius of Oscar the Grouch):
lessons from a life in feathers / Caroll Spinney with J Milligan.
p. cm.
ISBN 0-375-50781-7
1. Spinney, Caroll. 2. Entertainers—United States—Biography.
3. Sesame Street (Television program) I. Milligan, Jason. II. Title.
PN2287.S6644 A3 2003
791.45′028′092—dc21   2002032962
[B]

Printed in the United States of America on acid-free paper

24689753

First Edition

Book design by Casey Hampton

This book is dedicated to my wife,

DEBRA,

who is my everything,

and to my dear friend and boss,

JIM HENSON,

who is now exploring new worlds, no doubt.

Hold fast to dreams
For if dreams die
Life is a broken-wing bird
That cannot fly.

—LANGSTON HUGHES

CONTENTS

THE WISDOM OF BIG BIRD

(and the Dark Genius of Oscar the Grouch)

MY LIFE AS A BIRD

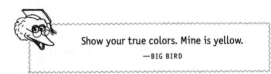

Show your true colors. Mine is yellow.
—BIG BIRD

The alarm goes off. The clock says 6:00 A.M., and my wife, Debra, and I wake up in our tiny studio apartment near Lincoln Center on the West Side of Manhattan.

It's a lovely day. For a moment I wish we were at our country home in New England. But it's a workday. It's time to go to Sesame Street.

I get up and put on the water for the tea.

For the first twenty-four years, *Sesame Street* was taped at studios in Manhattan and I would ride my bicycle to work. Then, in 1992, the show moved to the Kaufman Astoria Studios in Queens, and ever since I've been driven to and from work in a van. It's waiting for me at a quarter to eight in front of my building, and as we drive up West End Avenue, I wave to Debi, who hangs out our thirtieth-floor window and waves back.

Some days we stop to pick up Kevin Clash, who plays Elmo. We'll talk shop—about puppets, or the scripts for the day, or any special projects we're working on—and the thirty-minute ride goes pretty quickly. Soon we're across the Fifty-ninth Street Bridge and at the studio door.

I head right to the back of the huge building, to my dressing room, where I gather my prepared scripts for the first scenes. Previously, I have cut, folded, and abridged the pages down to a size that I can fit inside the Bird with me. Six or seven pages of script have to fit on a card that is only five by fifteen inches. Perfecting this technique has made me quite an origami artist. I sometimes spend as much as three or four hours preparing the scripts for a day, and although I've been offered help with this task, I feel that if I don't do it myself, it just won't be done right.

At two minutes to nine, I pull on Big Bird's feet and legs. They're basically a pair of pants made of orange-dyed fleece with the feet already attached, like hip boots or big "feetie" pajamas. A pair of my Hush Puppy loafers is built into the foam feet, which are covered in slippers when they're not actually seen on camera. The slippers protect the feet from getting dirty (children love to step on them while we work), and they are usually little characters in their own right, with eyes and ears, made by our clever puppet builders. My current pair is green, with floppy bunny ears.

At nine o'clock the speaker in my dressing room crackles and Adam Matalon, the stage manager, says, "We need the

Bird on the floor, if you're ready, Caroll." That's my cue to waddle out toward the set. In order not to trip over the big feet, I have to walk toes-out, which took me some years to learn to do naturally. I grab my folded scripts and walk past the soda machine and the coffee urns that are set up for the cast and crew, through the carpentry shop and the prop-building shop, past the control room, and onto Sesame Street in Studio G.

The set curves around itself, starting with the new Mail-It Shop and Hooper's Store on the left, followed by the Community Garden at the bend, the brownstone at 123 Sesame Street, and Oscar's trash can. Big Bird's nest area is around the next bend, and in the back of the studio is a large space for blue-screen or green-screen work, or sets for inserts like Bert and Ernie's apartment, the Count's Number of the Day, or musical numbers. It's always easy to see where we're working—it's the area surrounded by three large TV cameras and a lot of bright lights. When I get there, Chuck Tutino, who's been the head utility man for all the years we've done the

show, hands me my harness, or "electronic bra," as we refer to it. It has my tiny TV receiver and wireless microphone strapped into a halter-type rig. Chuck helps me Velcro it to my chest, and I'm ready to go.

The director leads a read-through of the scene. This is essentially our first rehearsal. We shoot so many scenes in a day and so many episodes a season that we don't have time to rehearse otherwise. During the read-through, we'll get the basic flow of the scene worked out and make any necessary changes to the script. Then we do it again for the cameras, and the director works out all the shots with the cameramen and the control room. When we've got it, somebody calls for "Feathers!" and Michael Schupbach, my assistant, brings out the puppet.

Kermit Love, who originally built Big Bird, would chastise anyone who called it a costume. "It's not a costume, it's a puppet," he would insist. "Do not say, 'Put on the costume,' say, 'Put on the puppet!' " But it's really a brilliant combination of the two, conceived by Jim Henson. Personally, I don't mind what it's called, and we'll refer to it interchangeably as "the Bird," "the feathers," "the costume," or even "the suit." The late Bob Myrum, who gave so much to *Sesame Street* as one of our directors, would always say, "Bird up the suit!"

The Bird sits on a two-by-four that is hinged, something like a catapult, so that it can bend over and the puppet can be removed.

"Ready?" asks Michael.

Everyone's waiting to begin, but I can't resist starting the running joke he and I have done for years.

"Hmm," I muse. "Do you have anything in blue for me today?"

He smiles. "Blue? No. Not today. I do have something in yellow. Will that do?"

"Yellow, eh? Well, I was really hoping for blue, but okay. I'll take the yellow one."

Michael picks up the Bird by grasping the lower beak while the upper beak rests on his hand. Then he grabs the puppet by a little tab of cloth that sticks out from the midst of the feathers. He holds it up, and I put my hands out in the diving position and walk right in. I hold my right arm up—that becomes the Bird's neck, and his head is in my hand. My little finger rests on a small lever that controls how wide his eyelids open. My thumb is in the lower jaw—that's how I make him speak. My left arm operates Big Bird's left wing and, via a piece of monofilament, his right wing too.

I have to wear a pair of ten-dollar drugstore reading glasses to see the tiny monitor that's inches from my eyes. This is the only view I have outside the Bird; it's the same third-person image that the TV cameras see, not the first-person view that we're all used to using to move around. My script is attached with Velcro to its place above the monitor. The stage manager counts us down: "Quiet on the set! In: Five! Four! Three! . . ."

I count the last two numbers silently in my head, and then—
"Action!" Big Bird greets the children at home, looking directly
at them through Frankie Biando's Camera One.

Playing Big Bird on *Sesame Street* has been my job for half
my lifetime. It is a fabulous career—more than I ever
hoped for, yet everything I believed it could be. Going to work
each day is a joy. The people I work with are tremendously talented and dedicated, and our mission—to educate and inspire
young children—is extremely motivating.

Watching *Sesame Street* teaches children lessons that get
them ready for school and the world. Being on *Sesame Street*
for thirty-four years has taught me a lot too. Through Big Bird
I've learned things that have changed my life, lessons that have
stayed with me even when I'm not in the puppet.

Big Bird has opened up new worlds to me. Because of him
I have made lifelong friends, overcome personal challenges,
traveled the world, performed on legendary stages, and found
my soul mate. I'm certain that being a bird has made me a better person, and I've tried to explain how in these chapters. I
hope that you too can benefit from what I've learned.

1

LISTEN TO YOURSELF

 To find out what one is fitted to do, and to secure
an opportunity to do it, is the key to happiness.
—JOHN DEWEY

D o you know how to get to *Sesame Street*? Some people have
found the way easily. I took a more scenic route.

When I was five, I saw a puppet show for the first time. It
was a version of "The Three Little Kittens." I was very concerned that since the little kittens had lost their mittens, they
would be punished by not being allowed to have any pie. Great
relief when in the end they got their pie after all!

After the show, the players came out front to take their
bows with their Steiff puppets, and I saw how a whole show
could be done with little things on your hands. This idea
stayed with me, and when I saw a puppet at a rummage sale a
couple of years later, I put him on my hand, and I knew that I
had to have him. The puppet was a monkey who had such a
large hole in his head that my finger wobbled around inside.
He cost a nickel.

I paired him up with a stuffed snake that my mother had made from green flannel. My family didn't have much money, so my mother would make us things like that for Christmas. With some orange crates, and curtains made from borrowed cloth, I fashioned a little puppet theater. I put a sign on our old barn: PUPPET SHOW! TWO CENTS! Sixteen people came and paid, and I had an audience.

I can't imagine what I did with only the monkey and the snake to keep people entertained for half an hour. But as I recall, everyone left with smiles on their faces, and I had thirty-two cents in my hand. In 1942, that was enough money to go to the movies three times. I already wanted to be a cartoonist when I grew up. After this show, I decided that I would also become a puppeteer. By that time I was eight years old.

It was my mother who really started my career. She secretly enlisted the help of my brother Donald to make my combination Christmas and birthday gifts (I'm only five hours younger than Christmas day) for my ninth year.

On Christmas morning, there was a mysterious something sitting next to the tree, hidden under a blanket. My mother whisked the cover away like a magician to reveal a beautiful puppet theater! Under the tree were eight puppets that she had built herself, in bright satiny colors that would look fine on the stage. With those puppets and that theater I had everything I needed to do a Punch and Judy show. My mother was from England, and she thought that Punch and Judy was a good way to get started in puppets.

The more I gave shows, the more I felt the power that one has when one is performing. All these people would sit in a room and listen to everything that I said. I did all the character voices: little girl voices, an old lady voice, and a ghost voice. The audience listened, and clapped at the end, and paid me to do it. What could be a better way to make a living than to perform? I knew that I would wind up in the world of entertainment.

Puppet shows were the way I made money during junior high and high school. When I needed money to go to art school, puppet shows helped me pay for my tuition. In college, I studied commercial art because it seemed like a secure way to make a living based on my talents and abilities. It has served me well over the years. But I always looked for my next chance to put on a show.

Before I could finish art school, I joined the Air Force because I was afraid I'd be drafted into the Army to fight in Korea. I found myself stationed in Las Vegas drawing large pictures of bombs for training aids. Due to the heat of the desert, we started our workdays at 5:30 A.M. and were finished by two in the afternoon. This left me with a lot of free time. Drawing advertising cards got me a job with a local television station. That was the foot in the door that I needed to show the station manager my idea for *Rascal Rabbit,* a puppet show for kids. Eventually, he gave me a weekly half-hour time slot. The television industry was only eight years old, and I was part of it.

Rascal Rabbit was only on the air for a couple of months before I was transferred to Germany, but once I tasted performing live for the camera, I knew that was what I wanted to do. There wasn't much difference, especially in the days before videotape, between putting on a live puppet show and putting on a television show. I got the same thrill, only magnified a thousand times because of the much greater exposure. Even though I couldn't see the audience, I knew they were there, and in far larger numbers than could fit in any theater. Having done it once, I knew I would find a way to get back to television again.

After the Air Force, I finished art school and looked around for work. I got into animation, which paid the bills but could be tedious work with no applause or glory. I knew I couldn't do it forever. A local Boston television station gave me a summer-replacement time slot, and I teamed up with a talented singer named Judy Valentine to create *The Judy and Goggle Show.* Though our ratings were good, we were not picked up in the fall. Instead, we were offered a weekly appearance on *Bozo's Big Top.* It wasn't what we wanted, but we took it. It was another chance to do puppets on TV, and *Bozo* was the most popular kids' show of its time. It had a huge live audience and took place in a circus tent set.

On *Bozo,* I played a number of characters that were hand puppets, as well as nine different walkabout characters. The full-body characters got me out of the puppet theater, onto the main floor, and into the audience. It's ironic that Jim Henson never saw my work on *Bozo,* because I'm sure that playing these full-body characters was valuable experience for the claustrophobic job of playing Big Bird. Being a puppet as well as a costume, Big Bird is much more technically demanding and expressive than the simple costumes we used on *Bozo,* but some of the skills I developed there were useful later. I learned to roller-skate in costume, which I'm sure helped me to skate as Big Bird and Bruno the Trashman.

I was on *Bozo* for ten years. Some of my characters were: Grandma Nellie, Bozo's clown grandmother, who constantly tried to hoodwink him; "Mr. Lion—the fastest draw alive," a ringmaster lion who drew animals out of kids' names; and Kookie, the boxing kangaroo, who could be knocked out by any little kid, because he had a glass jaw and always led with his chin.

As the years went on, and my work was on the air live three

days a week and on tape Sunday mornings, I slowly began to feel that my career wasn't really going anywhere. While what I was doing paid pretty well, it did not make me feel I had ever done anything really important. People study and work for years to become doctors, nurses, teachers, scientists—professions that add to the community and the nation. What was I doing? Working on the *Bozo* show as a bunch of sidekicks. It was schlock, and I was basically phoning it in. I wanted to do something more meaningful, but I didn't know what. All I knew was that it would be a TV show for kids and that it would involve puppets. So I decided to go see some puppet shows.

2

ASK HIM WHAT HE MEANS

Assumptions allow the best
in life to pass you by.
—JOHN SALES

was a member of the Puppeteers of America, an organization dedicated to the advancement of puppetry for amateur and professional puppeteers alike. They used to hold an annual weeklong festival of puppet shows from America and all over the world. In 1968 the festival was in St. Louis, Missouri, and I thought that if I went, I might gain some inspiration.

he previous festival I had attended was in 1963 at a small resort hotel in the Catskills. I had driven there in my troublesome Volkswagen bus with only fourteen dollars in my pocket. Too broke to register as a participant, I had to sneak in to all the shows. There were lots of hilarious acts with both hand puppets and marionettes. Jim Henson performed, and he introduced his wonderful dog puppet, Rowlf. The dog was so new, his ear, which was only pinned on, fell off during his performance. Rowlf spoke of his deep philosophy using one of his fleas to make a point.

"You know," he said, "life is funny sometimes. How you look at things often depends on your point of view. Let me demonstrate."

He searched his fur and looked satisfied when he found a flea.

"Take this flea. Now, to me, it's this tiny and annoying creature that I can barely see. But to him, I'm a towering mountain of a being, and he knows that I hold in my hand the power of life"—he placed the flea on the play board and bashed it with a closed fist—"or death!"

I didn't get to talk to Jim at all at that festival, but I was humbled by his talents.

One of the presentations at the St. Louis festival was a film on Richard Teschner, an Austrian puppeteer who died in 1948. He had worked with rod puppets, magnificent figures with porcelain faces and flowing gowns. His stories were mostly macabre, with scenes such as a mad scientist working in his laboratory with his Igor-type assistant.

Still, in spite of the strange stories, they were the most beautiful scenes I had ever seen done with puppets. I was moved by the last story, "There Goes My Heart." A mechanical man sits at an impressive puppet organ and begins to play. A little mechanical glass duck waddles in and sits, obviously enjoying the music. When the tune is finished, the robot reaches over and pats the duck on the head. The duck looks at the man with loving eyes, and the little duck's heart suddenly glows bright red through his glass body. Did Spielberg get his E.T. idea here?

Teschner's work inspired me, and somehow I got the idea to create kinetic scenery for a multimedia puppet show. Not only would the puppets have movement, but the backgrounds themselves would move in time with the action. I would draw the scenery and film it on an animation stand.

I thought that I might build a large hand-puppet stage with a background made of a special surface for rear-screen projection. On the screen, I would be able to project animations of anything I chose: puppets who were done in animation, moving backgrounds, all sorts of special effects not usually possible in normal puppet presentations. I thought that combining the media of film and live puppetry could bring a new dimension to puppet theater.

I wasn't officially performing in this festival, but fortunately for me, like many puppet festivals this one included something called "potpourri," in which anyone can start a show, whether he's booked or not. One night at midnight, a bunch of puppeteer friends and I decided to get a potpourri together. We started knocking on doors, anyplace we saw a light on, and called out, "Potpourri in fifteen minutes in the lobby!" Thirty or forty people came down, and we did a show.

My cat puppet, Picklepuss, was with me, and I did some ad-lib stuff, making fun of lip sync. I did a demonstration of bad lip-synching, first talking with Picklepuss's mouth not moving, then suddenly with his mouth moving too much, and it got big laughs. Some people from the audience came up to me the next day and asked if I had a larger show. I boldly told them I did and that it was an experiment combining film and puppets. They liked the idea and said they wanted to book me for the Puppeteers of America convention the following year. Now I had to actually make my show.

In Newton, Massachusetts, I had use of an Acme animation stand. For months I spent evenings drawing and filming my presentation and designing and building my theater. I had studied some of the works of the Canadian Film Board and had learned how to make an endless zoom-in to give the image of a bird flying through a swamp jungle. I constructed a puppet seagull that flew directly away from the audience, and the illusion of dimension and movement worked perfectly. I also created in animation some tall dancing cones that would suddenly take form as rod puppets that appeared to jump off the screen and then perform in front of their own filmed images.

The screen itself was the largest and most expensive element that I required. It was seven feet wide by three and a half feet high and cost two hundred fifty dollars. It was a fortune for me, but necessary to fulfill my vision. I already had the projectors—a slide projector and an RCA sixteen-millimeter film projector, which I set up on ladders behind the screen. Then I built an elaborate theater out of aluminum tubing, with beautiful black cloth sewn on over the framework. Because the screen was above the play board, the top of the thing was nine feet in the air. This forced me to work on my knees, because to work standing up would make it even higher, too high for most stages. I put down padding, and made knee switches to control the music and the projectors. I could run the entire show—all of the puppets, the sound, and the visuals—by myself, on my knees.

I was asked to perform my new show at a small regional puppet festival in Binghamton, New York. A good friend and neighbor, Ronny Chick, helped me build a large plywood box in which to transport the theater to Binghamton.

I believe it was in April 1969 that I first presented my new production. It went smoothly and I considered it a success.

I named the show *Picklepuss and Friends*. It featured Picklepuss, my puppet cat, as master of ceremonies. I was going to place the opening scene in a back alley, where Pick would emerge from a trash can with a fish bone on his head. There were so many elements to put together that I never got around to making the trash-can prop. Of course, Jim didn't know about this when he assigned Oscar to me.

Building this show was so exciting that it lifted me out of the Bozo miasma I had been dwelling in over the previous years. With this magic theater, I could mount any scene, with a background done either in art or in real photography.

I thought I was ready for the big audience at the national puppetry festival in Salt Lake City.

I assembled my stage and set up my projectors and my knee switches. I carefully set the theater spotlights so they'd illuminate my puppets but not throw any unwanted light on my movie screen. This was the one element that I could not control from inside my theater, and it had to be right from the start. Finally, all was set and I left to have supper.

It was showtime.

Just as I was going on, I was told that Jim Henson had arrived and was in my audience. Suddenly, the other thousand people in the hall vanished and he became *the* audience. I was both delighted and apprehensive. The curtains parted, revealing my large black velour puppet theater at center stage. I stepped out and briefly stated that I was presenting a new medium—live puppetry with active backgrounds on film, an experimental production that I hoped the audience would find interesting and entertaining. After some polite applause, I disappeared behind my stage, turned on my taped music, and pushed the knee switch to start my movie projector.

The theater lit up and I picked up my puppets. The routine was supposed to be a carefully choreographed dance. First, three white cones would appear on-screen. They were very shy, and they moved around cautiously to the music. Then I would bring on the two rod puppets I'd made out of Styrofoam cones from the flower shop, one in each hand. The cones on screen were afraid of the puppets at first, but all of a sudden, at the right spot in the music, the puppets would appear to jump onto the screen. Then all five cones would dance together. That was how it was supposed to happen.

I started the music and the film and looked up from below the screen. To my horror, a brilliant pool of light was washing out the entire picture! I couldn't see the images on-screen at all. A spotlight that wasn't on when I set up the stage was now blazing from the back. Who turned that on? I couldn't see my film to synchronize my movements or do any of the planned choreography with the figures. I tried a few things, but what could I do? I had to see what was happening on-screen to manipulate the puppets in time, and since I couldn't see anything, it was immediately a disaster. I lost the whole bit. All the little nuances and signals were gone, and the audience just saw cones randomly moving around to no purpose. It was a terrible start to the show. Worse, once the soundtrack was off, there was no way to get back in synch for the next act. And Jim Henson was in the audience!

I killed the music and cut the power to the projector, completely stopping my show. I could sense the audience's confusion. I stepped out and looked up to see where the spotlight was coming from.

There, up in the back, from among the small spots I had carefully aimed earlier, a large klieg light blasted onto my screen.

"Would you please turn off the big spot?" I shouted out into the dark hall, a prayer to the theater gods.

"We don't know how," answered a student operator.

"Why don't you look at all the switches that are on, and turn them to off until the big light goes off," I suggested, unable to hide the frustration in my voice.

"We don't know how."

Standing helpless at center stage, I was fully aware that this was not a show people would pay to see. And did I mention Jim Henson was in the audience?

I was desperate. "Does anyone in the audience have a rifle?" I implored.

This got a laugh.

The students shut off all the lights, and the only light onstage was from my slide projector behind the screen. Struggling to save the show in any way I could, I quickly ran back there and turned myself into a shadow puppet. I mimed pulling out my hair in frustration and screamed, "Aaaaugh!" This got an even bigger laugh. Then from the wings I heard, "Stop! Don't take another step back!" Inches behind me was a huge pit, twenty feet deep, where a section of the stage had been lowered. My show was a disaster, and now I had almost fallen to my death.

Eventually, the students fixed the lights and I recued my film and music for my big finale, the flying-bird scene. I managed to pull it off, and I got a big hand. When my show ended, I wanted to *really* disappear into the floor. I felt it was a total fiasco.

Then I heard a soft voice next to me say, "Hello."

It was Jim. He asked me to meet him in the lounge once I had finished putting my stuff away. What could he want?

I had met him only once, seven years before in Sturbridge, Massachusetts. My friend Gordon Bennett, a teacher and a puppeteer, had sponsored a regional puppet festival at Tantasqua High School. The Boston Area Guild of Puppetry sent out announcements to other guilds, and we were amazed and delighted that the Muppets had come. Jim and Jerry Juhl, a Muppets writer, gave a fifty-five-minute presentation. It was the most fascinating puppet show I have ever seen. A troop of wooden soldiers marched on under the command of a bellowing drill sergeant and went through a lot of drill moves. They ended up blowing him away with little puffs of smoke coming out of their little guns. And that was only one of eight scenes.

Then I gave my show "The Big Bad Dragon," followed by my snarky bird, Goggle, who would never cooperate and always ended up biting my nose. I would end his bit by going back behind my stage and when I couldn't get him to depart I would reach up with my left hand, grab him by the neck, and yank him off. Jim always liked physical moves with puppets like that.

Jim had come backstage, complimented me on my show, and then said, "Why don't you come down to New York and we can talk about the Muppets?"

I said that would be nice, and I thought, I'll do that, by gosh, maybe. But I never got around to it. I had mistakenly assumed that he just wanted to chat. When I got to know him better, I learned that Jim Henson never wanted to chat. He almost always wanted to work. If he said he wanted to talk about something, it meant that he wanted to do it. But I hadn't asked him what he meant. Now, in Utah, he wanted to talk to me again. I had a sense that this time I had better find out what he

wanted to talk about. I quickly stashed my show safely away and rushed to the lounge.

He sat on a low couch, in a way only Jim seemed to sit. His whole back was on the seat with his head bent forward and his long legs halfway across the floor.

"I saw your show," he said. "I liked what you were *trying* to do."

I discovered I could smile again. He recounted some of his own disasters, including driving a hundred miles to do a show and finding he'd left the all-important audiotape back in the workshop.

Then he said, "Why don't you come down to New York and talk about the Muppets?"

This time, amazed at this déjà vu moment, I asked him to clarify. "What do you mean by 'talk about the Muppets'?"

"I mean, would you like to work for me?" he replied.

I could hardly believe my ears. This was bigger than anything I had hoped would come of the festivals. My mind reeled at this fabulous turn of events, a chance I had dreamed of for what seemed my whole life.

He told me that he was working with the producers of a new, experimental show for kids called *Sesame Street* and had done some puppetry for them in their two trial shows. He and Frank Oz had already created Ernie and Bert, who tested very well, but they were too busy to spend every day at the studio. The show had as its set a very realistic city street, and it needed more fantasy. Jim had given the problem a lot of thought and came up with two new characters that one person could perform—a large bird and a Grouch.

Of course, I said I'd do it. I told him that as soon as I was back on the East Coast, I'd drive down to New York, to "talk about the Muppets."

3

TAKE A PAY CUT

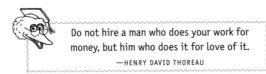

Do not hire a man who does your work for
money, but him who does it for love of it.
—HENRY DAVID THOREAU

Artistically, I've had three main heroes in my life: Walt
Disney, whose very name has brought delightful images
to my mind since I was a child; Andrew Wyeth, who I always
felt painted just for me; and Jim Henson. Now I was headed to
New York to meet with my third hero.

As I drove down to New York from my home in New
England, my mind was full of questions. What would I actually do with the Muppets? In all the bits I had ever seen them
perform, that fabulous troupe was way-out and unique. They
showed up regularly on *The Ed Sullivan Show* and always blew
me away with incredible surprise endings. One of my favorite
bits featured an early version of Kermit the Frog happily pan-
tomiming to the song "I've Grown Accustomed to Your Face."
Next to him is a furry character whose head is covered with a
cloth that has a cute feminine face drawn on it. As Kermit

sings, he doesn't notice the creature eating the cloth, causing the face to crumple and disappear into her gaping mouth. Kermit suddenly sees this, does a double take, and is promptly eaten by the faceless monster.

Most of my impressions of what the Muppets did were as macabre as this example. I had never worked in this style. Would I be doing things like that? Would I be good enough to be a real Muppeteer? And what would the Muppets be doing for *Sesame Street,* a new educational program being developed to reach inner-city children?

I was also thinking about more mundane, practical matters. What would it be like to have a job in New York City? I'd always been a little intimidated by big, dirty New York. I was used to working in Boston, which was a cute little city by comparison. Besides, although Boston was seventy miles from my home, I could commute back and forth daily. New York was over 150 miles away, too far to drive twice a day.

I entered the city, and I made my way to 227 East Sixty-seventh Street. Years ago it had been a carriage house. Now next to the door was a small hand-lettered sign painted by Jim Henson himself. It read: "The Muppets," and in smaller print: "Someday this sign will be replaced by a real one, maybe."

I rang the doorbell and the latch buzzed. I started up the long, steep staircase, and Jim appeared way up at the top.

"Keep coming!" he shouted. At a landing I looked to the right and saw several puppets, in various stages of completion, lying on worktables.

"That's our workshop," he explained.

At last, at the top, he showed me his neatly designed screening room. At that time everything was on sixteen-millimeter film. Videotape would come later. The next room was Jim's unique office. An imposing mahogany table with carved lions for legs stood as his desk. Over the fireplace hung a majestic wire-and-paper moose head looking down on us, a gift a friend had made for him.

We sat together, and Jim outlined what he thought my job would be. He thought I could play two characters he was developing. "I picture making Big Bird a large feathered bird, who is very funny and very silly," he explained. "Oscar will be a purple Grouch, a furry creature that lives in a pile of litter and trash in the gutter."

I tried to picture these characters. A huge, silly bird and a creature who lives in the trash? Well, all the Muppets I had seen were quite strange, so why not these?

I wondered what the Bird and Oscar would actually do, as there were no scripts available at this point. I had no idea how they would fit in the show, or what voices I would use. Still, I was confident I could learn. I *had* to do this! I was being asked to work for someone who, in my mind, was the greatest puppeteer in history. This show *had* to work.

The telephone rang, and Jim said he had to spend some time on the call. He told me that while I waited I could go through the cardboard file cabinets that lined the walls. They turned out to hold an amazing assortment of puppets. I found a drawer of old Kermit puppets, made from the coat Jim's mother used to wear. There was a set of characters from *The Wizard of Id,* Johnny Parker's comic strip, for a series that didn't make it to television. Too bad. They looked great.

Jim returned and announced it was time for lunch. "Do you like seafood?" he asked. I said that I did and we walked up the block to a restaurant named Oscar's. A story circulated in later years among the *Sesame* writers that Oscar's restaurant had a very grouchy waiter and Jim got the idea for the character from him. If that was true, Jim never mentioned it to me, even as I was given the Grouch assignment. However, I do believe that's where Jim came up with Oscar's name.

Back at the workshop, Jim suggested we try doing some puppets together.

I gulped at the prospect of working with a true master. I hadn't been nervous about performing in years, but now I was almost shaking.

He opened a drawer and there were three Rowlf the dogs looking up at us. Since I had first seen him, Rowlf had become a regular on *The Jimmy Dean Show* and later would play piano on *The Muppet Show.* "Woof! Woof!" Jim brought Rowlf to life as we stood in front of one of many work mirrors. "Hello there," said Rowlf. I tried a Rowlf. I had my Rowlf talk to his Rowlf. We worked for a while, Jim's relaxed nature putting me at ease.

Jim pointed out that I was moving the top of Rowlf's head up and down along with the lower jaw. "We don't move our skull when we talk. Only the jaw moves." That would be one's thumb in the puppet's mouth. The four fingers on top should hold steady. He demonstrated by amusingly bouncing his whole head up and down as he explained this point of manipulation. That was probably the only lesson I got from Jim prior to actually performing. Future lessons came as I worked—on-the-job training.

It was all settled except for one point—money. I asked what I could expect to earn.

Jim looked thoughtful and raised a finger. "We have a tradition," he stated.

I smiled. Who doesn't like a nice tradition?

"What is it?" I asked.

"You won't get paid much," he said.

That wasn't at all what I'd expected to hear. After all, I was joining the Muppets, the preeminent puppet troupe in the world. Wouldn't I get rich quick? His first offer was two hundred dollars a week. I was making almost that much a day in Boston on *Bozo's Big Top.* Although I was delighted at the chance to perform on this new, high-profile educational television program, I had assumed I would earn more than I did on *Bozo,* not less. Certainly, having to live half the year in New York City would be expensive.

Jim allowed that he really had no idea what people earned at that time. We finally came to an agreement that would earn me seven thousand dollars a year less than I made in Boston.

I would take a pay cut, but at last I would become a Muppeteer.

As I drove home, I thought about what had just happened. I had a feeling that my life would never be the same, and that this was the opportunity I had been looking for, the one I'd been training for all my life. I knew that Big Bird was a big deal. I had no idea how big he would become.

4

FIND YOUR INNER BIRD

No bird soars too high
if he soars with his own wings.
—WILLIAM BLAKE

s the first day of *Sesame Street* production got closer, I began to think about what kind of character Big Bird could be.

When I first met with Jim at his office, I asked him, "What do you think he's like? How do you want me to play Big Bird?"

Jim's idea was to have him be goofy and a little dumb. For instance, because Big Bird is so tall, when he'd enter a scene he'd bump his neck into the top of a doorway and then shake his fist and say, "Stupid door!"

But what kind of voice did Jim want? Like a parrot? Or a falsetto bird voice?

Jim thought about it. "Maybe like Mickey Mouse's pal Goofy. Or maybe like Mortimer Snerd" (Edgar Bergen's country yokel, designed to contrast with his wise-guy character, Charlie McCarthy). "When you did the show I saw in Salt

Lake City, I liked the voice you used for your character Pistachio."

Pistachio did sound a lot like Mortimer Snerd. (He also sounded very close to a certain purple dinosaur I won't name who became quite popular years later). Jim said, "I think that would be a good voice, because I think of Big Bird as kind of a yokel, a silly guy from the country."

He also told me that I should go with what I felt came from the puppet, once it had been built. Jim liked to work that way. He had faith in his puppeteers and he had faith in his puppets—the puppet itself often has the power to suggest its character to the puppeteer. Jim was so busy at the time, working on Ernie and Bert, building Big Bird and Oscar, and developing films for the show, that he hadn't gone any further than designing the puppets and deciding that Oscar would be grouchy.

In the first episode of *Sesame Street,* Big Bird walked in and saw a little girl riding on Gordon's shoulders. In his yokel voice, Big Bird said, "Wow! You're the tallest little girl I've ever seen!"

For the first few weeks he would only appear for a minute or two in each show. You could always tell Big Bird was arriving by the crash of trash cans that he would trip over as he came through a door in the fence. "Well, here I am!" he drawled each time.

They kept writing for him like he was the village idiot. He didn't have a clue about anything, and it seemed that he had no real purpose on the show except as a comic diversion. Certainly, he had no educational value.

That first season, *Sesame Street* was rapidly evolving. The writers weren't very far ahead on the scripts, and they gradually started including Big Bird more and giving him more things to do. After about a month Jeff Moss, the head writer, sent along a script that initiated a very important change for the Bird. It called for him to want to visit a day-care center. A lot of children were going inside—it looked like fun—and he wondered why he couldn't go in as well. Big Bird was supposed to put up a big fuss until he was included.

When I got this script, I thought, Why would the village idiot want to go to day care? What would happen if he did go? And who would want that kind of big weirdo hanging around with their children? But if he were a child, he could go to day care and play with other kids. Most important, if Big Bird were a child, children watching the show could better identify with him. I decided that I should really be playing him as a kid, rather than as a yokel.

I dropped all aspects of the hillbilly accent and made his voice lighter and higher, so that he sounded more childlike. When he came to the part in the script where he couldn't go into the day-care center, he jumped up and down and threw a tantrum. It felt very natural, and I knew that suddenly I had a real, human, complex character to work with. He was the too-big kid, much as I had been the too-little kid when I was his age. I suggested that we think of him as a child first learning to read and learning the alphabet, like our audience. That made him about four and a half. Everyone agreed that was a good idea, and we went ahead with it.

Big Bird gets quite a bit of mail. In the early years of *Sesame Street* I answered a lot of the letters myself. I did my best to keep up with it but soon fell far behind. Big Bird was becoming too popular for me to manage his correspondence. The show's public relations department took over but still forwarded a number of the more interesting letters for me to read.

One letter was from the mother of a four-year-old boy on a farm in Saskatoon, Saskatchewan. Her older children went off to school each day, and the youngest had to stay at home with no other kids around. "The other day I heard Joshua crying," she wrote. "I went into the living room where he was watching *Sesame Street*. On that episode, Big Bird was feeling very sad for himself, sniffling because all the other kids were older than he and had gone off to school. Big Bird was alone, with no one to play with. Joshua said that 'Big Bird is just like me. He has no one to play with, too!' "

At the time I was forty-three, a grown man, yet I was able to play a child that a four-year-old could identify with and feel was his friend. The country-yokel Bird could not have had that effect on a child.

If Big Bird had remained the original dumb, goofy character, he would not be on the show today. Once he became somebody that children could relate to, in spite of his absurd appearance and his incredible height, they came to feel like he was their friend. His age has fluctuated over the years—he grew a little older and now he's getting younger again—but once Big Bird became a child, the children watching came to love him.

5

TRY ADDING MORE FEATHERS

 Do not be too timid and squeamish about
your actions. All life is an experiment.
—RALPH WALDO EMERSON

A few days after Jim hired me, work began on building the Big Bird puppet. Arriving at the Muppet workshop on East Sixty-seventh Street on a Monday morning for measurements, I had no idea what to expect. Waiting for me were Don Sahlin, Jim's head puppet builder, along with puppet builder Caroly Wilcox and the incredible Kermit Love, a man well known for his costuming of many of George Balanchine's ballets.

The Big Bird puppet was based on a brilliant idea that I believe is a Jim Henson original: his head is a sophisticated hand puppet, while his neck, body, and legs are a costume that the puppeteer wears over his body.

The first application of this idea was the La Choy Dragon, a puppet that Jim built for a series of commercials seen in the sixties. The dragon worked exactly as the Bird does. Frank Oz manipulated the puppet, and Jim did the voice.

The dragon would enter a kitchen and shout, "Hi! I'm the La Choy Dragon!" Touting the convenience of canned chop suey, he would destroy the kitchen as he heated up a can of food by breathing real fire on it, from a flamethrower inside the suit. He'd torch the cabinets, then smash the counters to smithereens with his powerful tail.

Frank hated being inside the foam plastic suit, and when he was offered the chance to play Big Bird, he emphatically declined: "No more suits!" He was too busy to work on the show every day anyway, which is why Jim had to find someone else to do it—me.

Jim was quite an artist, and he had drawn a sketch of how he wanted Big Bird to look. It was up to the puppet builders to figure out how to actually make the thing. Don began working on the head, while Kermit took my measurements.

Jim and Kermit had many conversations about the construction and feathering of the Bird. This is how they finally decided to build him: the body is formed by a series of hoops held together by cloth netting. They function the way whalebone was used for corsets and hoop skirts in earlier times. Kermit said that the Bird is built "like a tutu." They bought lots of American turkey feathers, which were dyed, fastened together in clusters of five, then glued to the netting with a hot-glue gun. For some reason the feathers were glued on with the back facing out. They started at the bottom and added the feathers in layers to "shingle" them up to the Bird's head. As a result, the original Big Bird ended up looking very raggedy.

Meanwhile, Don Sahlin was building the head. The skull was formed by half of a hard plastic ball, to which the beak was attached. The beak was constructed around a maple core, with balsa wood forming its shape. Big Bird's eyes were made from plastic balls with a clockworklike cluster of gears inside that allowed me to control his expressions. The first version of the head featured very sad-looking eyelids with practically no feathers above them, which made the Bird appear rather brainless and pathetic, like a sad child who can't find his mother.

Big Bird's first set of feet had very pointy toes. They were made around a pair of my boots, which had tall heels. The orange fleece leggings were sewn to the feet and held up over my shorts with a belt and straps. The first version of the Bird was about seven feet, ten inches tall.

One of Jim's original ideas was to have the puppeteer in the rig stand backward and face the Bird's head behind him. That way, Big Bird's knees would bend the way a real bird's do, rather than the way a human's legs bend. Fortunately, Jim abandoned that idea, or I could have spent over thirty years walking around backward.

After about a month of construction, it was time to try on the Bird. I donned the legs, and the huge puppet was lifted by the beak and bottom hoop, then lowered over me. I reached up, slid my left arm into the left wing and my right arm and hand up into the head. There was a big mirror in the workshop, and I turned to face it, peeking through a tiny hole made by removing a few feathers from Big Bird's chest. I was startled by the image in the glass. Big Bird was the ugliest puppet I had ever seen.

Sesame Street was going to begin taping the following week. With no time to improve the Bird, he was declared ready. He greeted the world on the first episode of the show.

Fortunately, the Muppets have always had a great spirit of constant innovation and evolution. Jim never considered anything to be "done," and this attitude was pervasive throughout the organization. Everything could always be improved—and was, including Big Bird.

Kermit Love, though he could be the most frustrating man I knew, was a perfectionist and a brilliant craftsman. He thought the original Bird looked pathetic and said so. He had several ideas for how he could make the Bird look and work better. When Big Bird was asked to be a presenter at the Emmy Awards in 1970, Jim acceded to Kermit's wishes.

The original puppet gave me no way to move the right arm. It was pinned to his side, motionless, until Kermit came up with this simple innovation: a piece of monofilament that runs from my left arm through a little plastic ring right under the chin and down to the right arm. This way, when I pull down on the left arm, the right arm moves up. Now both his arms could have life.

Jim also let Kermit put more feathers on top of Big Bird's head and change his eye design.

When the Bird's head was removed from his traveling box, I was amazed at the transformation. His sad-looking eyelids had been completely altered. Now I would have control over the eyes' expression. They were full of life and could look interested or surprised, whatever was needed. And instead of having only a few small topknot feathers above the eyes, his head was now full of feathers and enormous, the size of a bushel basket.

After the show Jim came backstage and agreed with Kermit that the Bird looked better with feathers above his eyes, but he added, "Take some off, please. Now his head is too huge!"

It wasn't just the Bird that changed the first season. The show was conceived of as an experiment, and like any experiment, it required a lot of trial and error, especially during the first year.

When Bob Myrum was hired, our show suddenly shone much brighter. Bob was a big bearded, shaggy bear of a man who wore tweed jackets and thick wool ties, and always had a cup of coffee in his hand. Jon Stone, one of the show's creators, had been Bob's roommate at Yale.

His first major contribution to the show was to bend the street. We had started with a straight sidewalk and all the buildings in a row. All camera shots had to be from out in the "street." With the street curving around, we had more camera angles and a new "outdoor" part of the set next to Hooper's Store.

In the original puppet, I had to perform the Bird virtually blind. To get a glimpse of a monitor, I could only peek between the feathers. I'd often stumble over things, bump into walls and parts of the set, and walk off camera in the wrong direction. Bob noticed my difficulties and came up with a solution.

"Can't we get one of those tiny TVs, put it inside the Bird puppet, set up a small transmitter, and send him a picture in there?" he asked.

Walt Rouffer, our television technician, said, "Sure, we can do that."

The moment I had the monitor inside the Bird, my performances became much better. I had room in the puppet to look down on the tiny picture and see what the Bird was doing. I see the same picture the viewer sees, not the world from the Bird's point of view, as many people assume. I can see if the Bird is looking at the other players or right into the camera's lens when he talks directly to the kids at home.

By the beginning of the second season, the Bird puppet looked like the one we use today. The original Big Bird was a light lemon yellow, and he had light flares streaming behind him as he moved across the screen. The new, perfected Bird had feathers that were double-dipped, yellow orange at the base and lighter yellow at the tip, which looked marvelous with the new cameras the show was using. The feathers were attached to the frame and netting much more beautifully and the head looked much handsomer, with the right amount of feathers on top, better eyes, and a more shapely neck. He grew a few inches from these improvements to his current eight feet two. The original puppet now seemed like Big Bird's ragbag cousin from the sticks.

esame Street was on-the-job-training for everyone, and Jim Henson and our talented producers really encouraged us all to evolve and innovate as we went along. If we hadn't, we'd probably have been off the air by the early seventies. And Big Bird would have remained shabby and ugly, not the beautiful puppet he has become.

The producers, directors, writers, and craftspeople never stop coming up with new ideas. I tried the new LCD screens, which are larger than my tube monitor and in color, but I find that if I don't look at them straight on, I can't see anything. Sometimes it's better to stick with what works than to go with new for the sake of newness. That's part of the learning process.

Even now the experiment continues. When we began in 1969, there were only three major networks, PBS, and a few independent stations. There were very few children's programs on television. We had almost no competition.

That was over thirty years ago, and much has changed since then. Today there are literally hundreds of channels to watch and many children's shows on all day long. In the early years we gave no thought to ratings, but with such immense competition of late, we found *Sesame* starting to lose popularity. The producers went back to tuning the experiment.

When *Sesame Street* began, it was discovered that young children paid a lot of attention to commercials, with their catchy songs and exciting visuals. Using *Laugh-In* as a model, we adopted a "magazine" format, with lots of short segments following one after the other. New research shows that kids respond well to repetition, predictability, and narrative, and the producers decided to change the formula of *Sesame* to give each episode a consistent structure. The thirty-third season, which aired in 2002, featured this new format. It was a hit with our young audience, and viewership increased 31 percent over the previous season. Research felt even more tweaking was necessary, and the thirty-fourth season reflects those changes. The world has changed a lot since 1969, and *Sesame Street* has had to change with it to stay relevant in the twenty-first century.

Sesame Street had been presented from the start as an experiment in children's television. Experiment is what we've been doing, and I believe we always will.

6

BECOME WHO YOU ALWAYS WERE

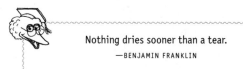

Nothing dries sooner than a tear.
—BENJAMIN FRANKLIN

One thing I love about performing on television is that once we start a scene, we often won't stop until the scene is over. Sometimes we shoot for five minutes straight, moving around the set with the cameras following the action. When that happens, I get lost in what I'm doing and I find that Big Bird lives, that I'm living the Bird's life.

Big Bird, like most of us, is not totally secure. He is a very emotional character, and when I'm living his life, I find myself experiencing the same wide range of emotions that he does. I feel his disappointments, his triumphs, his sadness, and his joy. When we're working on a long scene and Big Bird really starts to live, that's the greatest fun of the job for me.

Jerry Nelson, the original puppeteer of Mr. Snuffleupagus, and I once had a scene in which Big Bird tells Snuffy that they can't be friends anymore. This took place in the days when

only Big Bird ever saw Snuffy and the grown-ups on the show told Big Bird that his friend was a figment of his imagination. In this scene Big Bird came to accept this and decided that if Snuffy wasn't real, they couldn't be real friends.

The two characters become distraught and burst into tears as they hug good-bye. Then Big Bird notices that his feathers are wet from Snuffy's giant teardrops. He reasons that if the tears are real, then Snuffy must be real too. They decide that they can be friends again after all.

When Jerry and I got out of our puppets, both of our faces were streaked with our own real tears. We got so into the feelings of the scene, and the feeling of having to say good-bye to an old friend, that we were both crying inside the puppets as we worked.

As I perform, there are a lot of physical, practical things I have to worry about. I have to study the tiny picture in my monitor to make sure Big Bird is looking at the right spot and walking in the right direction. I'm committing as much of the script to memory as I can, so I don't have to read my lines on the pages around my monitor. My right arm will start to tire after a while, and I have to ignore the aches and pains to keep Big Bird's head up and looking alive. But after so many years, working the puppet has become something like touch typing. I don't have to think about it too much, and I can concentrate on expressing what Big Bird is thinking and feeling. I didn't create the puppet, and I don't write the scripts, but I guess what I do is bring Big Bird his soul.

It's like Big Bird is the actor and he expresses himself when I say his lines. He puts his own self into it. He's the child that I wanted to be, the kind of person I think we all should be. Someone once said to me, "If you're lucky, you become who you always really were." I am lucky. I think Big Bird has let me become who I always was.

7

LISTEN TO YOUR CABBIE

Too bad all the people who know how to run the country
are busy driving taxicabs and cutting hair.
—GEORGE BURNS

When Jim approached me about playing Big Bird, he also had me in mind for another new character, a Grouch named Oscar.

At first Jim told me that Oscar was going to be purple and live in a pile of trash in the gutter. In the late sixties New York was far messier than it is now, and it wasn't uncommon to step over paper, cans, and heaps of garbage in the streets. But Jim discovered that the studio had no trapdoors that would allow a puppeteer to work from under the floor, so the pile-of-trash idea wouldn't work. He switched Oscar's home to a trash can among some wooden crates, which remains a fixture on the set to this day.

Jim wanted to see me work the puppet and to hear the voice I would use before he officially cast me as Oscar. He asked me to meet with him and Don Sahlin on the set on the Friday before the first episode began taping.

My big worry was that I didn't know how Oscar should sound. I hadn't even seen the puppet yet, and though I had been experimenting with voices for this grumpy character, I still didn't have one that satisfied me. I had never done a character like Oscar, and I didn't feel any of my voices sounded like the Muppets that I was used to hearing.

I took a taxi to the meeting, and as I got in, the cabdriver turned his head around to look at me. He was the stereotypical cabbie of the time—a guy in his forties from the Bronx wearing a tweed cap with a little brim—and he kind of growled out of the corner of his mouth, "Where to, Mac?"

Wow, that's a great voice, I thought. It would be perfect for Oscar!

Who could be more of a Grouch than a cabdriver from the Bronx? I had the ideal model for my new character.

I kept repeating, "Where to, Mac?" to myself to lock the sound and attitude in my mind, as the driver went on and on, colorfully expressing his opinion of Mayor Lindsey with a lot of four-letter words.

The studio that *Sesame Street* started out in was called Teletape. It was a converted RKO movie theater at Eighty-first and Broadway. They had leveled the floor where the audience used to sit, and the old proscenium and domed ceiling could still be seen above the new lighting grids and catwalks.

The set represented a realistic section of a city street; it had a straight sidewalk going all the way across, an empty storefront, a tenement, Mr. Hooper's store, an alleyway with a board fence, the famous brownstone at 123 Sesame Street, and at its side, Oscar's messy domain. To this day I've wondered why Oscar's neighbors would put up with such a hideous pile of junk in their midst.

Jim and Don walked in, and I finally met the Grouch when Don pulled him out of an overnight bag. Instead of being purple, as Jim had described the puppet to me, he was dark orange. The first Oscar was simply constructed, with the head stitched onto a cotton work glove. My thumb operated the jaw, and the fingertips were sewn to the top of the mouth. When I tried him on, I found he was rather floppy and formless.

I knelt behind the cutaway trash can and attempted to put Oscar up to the opening. The prop builders had had no previous experience with puppets and had built the trash can with such a small opening that I couldn't get my right arm in at all. I could get my left arm up there, so I tried Oscar on my left hand. He was built on a right-hand glove, and now the thumb was on the wrong side. When I forced my left thumb in, it twisted Oscar's mouth into a permanent sneer.

Jim said we'd have to make do with the situation as it was for a while, until they got a chance to rebuild the trash can.

"Well, let's see what you're going to do with him," said Jim.

This was it. Would Jim like it? He was, after all, the king of the whole puppet world, and now with Oscar such a pathetic sight and me having to use my left arm, would what I did be good enough?

"Stand in front of the can and knock on the lid, and I'll have Oscar come up and say something," I suggested.

Jim knocked. I pulled the lever and the lid flew up. I was still repeating "Where to, Mac?" in my head. I hoped I had the right voice.

"Get away from my trash can!" growled Oscar.

I couldn't see Jim from inside, but I heard him say, "That'll do fine."

BE A GROUCH

Oscar is a complicated character. He's sometimes misunderstood, even by the writers and people who work on the show. He's not a villain, not horrible, not into spiders and ghoulish stuff, and although he can be rude and mean, he fundamentally has got a heart of gold. He's just a Grouch, that's all. He's a forty-three-year-old cabdriver from the Bronx. I think of him as a perfectionist, like the people who breed new kinds of roses; he's into his thing, he's often alone, and when somebody intrudes on him, naturally he gets grouchy. Of course, his thing is trash, not roses, but it's the same idea.

There's a story that a friend of mine told me, right after I got out of the Air Force in the late fifties, that I think helps define Oscar's character. I'd met Gunther Pfaff at the little film company in Boston where we both worked. He was from

southern Germany, and as a child he had had two neighbors: a very self-righteous woman on one side and a very grouchy man on the other. The woman told everyone how important and good she was because she always went to church and was very pious. The man was such a grouch that if your ball landed on his side of the fence, you would never get it back.

As World War II was nearing its end, food distribution stopped in Germany and people were forced to go to the dump to look for something to eat. Gunther and the man from next door both spotted a dented can of peaches at the same second, but the man stepped back as the little boy rushed for it. "You take it," he said. "You're probably hungrier than I am." Then the pious woman screeched like a Valkyrie, pried the can out of Gunther's fingers, and ran home with it. She was the "proper" person, but the grouch let the child have the food. That's what Oscar would do. As grouchy as he is, he would always let a hungry kid eat before he did.

O scar is a lot of fun to play. He's such a paradox; he gets so much enjoyment out of being miserable. That's what keeps him living on Sesame Street. All the cooperative, friendly people, kids, and monsters annoy him so much, he's in heaven. I used to do a quick routine with him that went like this:

You know what I can't stand? I hate when people do things that make me happy. Give me a present of some trash, and I'm happy. But I don't like being happy . . . so that makes me miserable. But I like being miserable, so that makes me happy . . . but I'm a Grouch, and I don't like being happy. I like being miserable! But being miserable makes me happy, which makes me miserable, and I like that, so I'm happy, which makes me unhappy . . . I'm a mess!

It's that dichotomy that makes Oscar so interesting, and so immensely satisfying to play; he's tough, he's smart, and, I discovered, he's cool. I've never been cool, but I think it's like Henry Winkler must have felt playing the Fonz on *Happy Days*. Henry was a nerd, like me, but when he'd come in as the Fonz, the audience would cheer and say, "Yay! He's so cool!"

He was still Henry Winkler with his heart of gold, but he was wearing a leather jacket and playing a tough guy. Oscar does that for me in a way. He generally thinks the opposite of the way I think, at least on the surface, but he gets to say exactly what he wants to say. He tells the truth, even when he probably shouldn't. The thing I always try to do is to make sure that his humanity comes through. I think kids get that.

Sometimes I put Oscar on to entertain people. I'll say something myself, and because he now has the power of life, he'll turn and glower at me and deliver an awful put-down. What amazes me is that I don't plan what he's going to say in advance. As soon as I hear myself say something, I know what Oscar will think about it and what he'll say in response. He doesn't think the way I think at all. I'm dealing with a mental entity who isn't me, even though I'm empowering him. Oscar has taught me the power of the puppet.

And I'll say this: after playing Big Bird all day, it is almost therapeutic to switch to Oscar, to live awhile with the exact opposite attitude about life.

BE FLEXIBLE

About a month after *Sesame* started taping, Don Sahlin had time to rebuild Oscar. I went to the Muppet workshop to meet Jim Henson and Don and help them design the new puppet. Jim was never sentimental about the puppets, and neither was Don. Jim just started ripping Oscar apart to reuse the material, which actually came from a bath mat dyed orange. I was horrified—*Sesame Street* was already a hit, and I felt like the first Oscar puppet could wind up in a museum someday. Jim and Don didn't care. They had the puppet stripped down in a few minutes and were thinking about how to build another one. "Let's keep the eyebrows," I suggested, and we did. In fact, to this day Oscar still has the eyebrows from the original orange Oscar.

The Oscar that everybody knows was built for an appearance on *The Flip Wilson Show.* When taping began, in July

1970, we opened Oscar's travel box and there he was—bright green. The last time I'd seen him, he'd been orange. At the end of the first season Jim Henson had changed his mind again and had the puppet rebuilt in green fur, with a differently shaped head. I quickly got used to it, and we went to work.

Dave Connell, who was president of Children's Television Workshop at the time, came out the second week of production on *Flip Wilson* to see what we'd taped. We'd done a lot of work in expensive Hollywood style, with lots of singing and dancing and skits. When Flip knocked on the trash can and this green thing popped out, Dave was quite upset. "What the hell is that? How can he be green?"

I told him, "Jim wanted him green."

"He didn't talk to us about it!" Dave protested. "We didn't give him permission for that! What can we do?"

They couldn't do anything. It was too late to stop them from using the green Oscar on the *Flip* show, and when the second season of *Sesame* started, we used the green Oscar for that too. He's been green ever since. Oscar's excuse for changing color was that he had gone on vacation in Swamp Mushy Muddy and it was so damp that he turned green overnight.

Oscar works the way most of the Muppets do—my thumb goes in the lower jaw and the rest of my fingers are in the upper jaw. My middle finger grabs a little white plastic ring. When I pull it back, it makes both his eyelids go up. Since his eyes won't close completely, when I want him to sleep I tip his head down so the whites of his eyes are hidden. He's a fabulously flexible puppet, due to his soft mouth and head. Unlike Big Bird, whose hard beak really only allows expression through camera angle, Oscar can actually change his expression. For example, by pushing my thumb forward, jutting his jaw out, and tipping his head down, I give him a big grin. If I pull my thumb back, he can quickly become aghast or frown in misery.

After the first couple of years the puppet builders went to repair Oscar and discovered that the foam rubber in his head had rotted away and a leather strap that was attached to his jaw had broken. This gave his mouth a nice, natural twist. They decided that rather than fix it, they would stabilize it so that the puppet wouldn't deteriorate further. Whenever they work on him, they try not to clean him too much. A clean Grouch just doesn't look right. Oscar's fur has to be matted and dirty for him to look good.

Oscar spends most of his time in his trash can, and why not, considering all the things that he's got in there—a crystal ballroom, elephants, a goat, a pig, a swimming pool, and even a racetrack—but there have been occasions when a mobile Oscar was needed for a particular scene. The first time he got to move around was when one of the writers had the idea of cutting the bottom out of the can and making legs out of Oscar's green fur. A little person would be needed to get in this costume, and the man for the job was Hervé Villechaize, whom I got to know. Later Hervé because famous for the role of Tattoo on *Fantasy Island,* but I had actually first seen him in a very strange play at Manhattan's La MaMa Theater, in which he was riding around on a tall, skinny guy who was making chicken sounds. Hervé was an intellectual, very thoughtful, and quite an artist. He played Oscar's legs in a number of *Sesame* shows and in the Hawaii episodes we did in 1978. He would be in the costume, and I would do Oscar's dialogue in voice-over. It was fun for us and a great way to get Oscar away from Sesame Street and into new situations.

As *Sesame Street* became something of an institution, we began to do live concerts and tour around the country. At first we couldn't use Oscar on the road, because there was no good way to get him out onto the stage. Then, while watching *The Gong Show,* I saw something that gave me an idea. A woman came out playing two characters at once—a clown pushing a baby carriage. Her head was in the pram, dressed up as the baby. Her legs were the clown's legs, and the rest of the clown was a puppet that she operated with her hands.

I designed a large puppet with a very Muppet-style head and face, a little like a burly Bert. The folks at the Muppet workshop built him, and they did a fantastic job. They made a huge, heavily padded pair of pants and big leather workboots, about size 22. The body was built to be put on over my head. He had big fake arms, which held the bails of the trash can. It looked like a real steel can but actually was made of plastic. My arms went into an opening in the back of the can and into the Oscar puppet. I named the trashman Bruno.

I have to say that the illusion was startling. I kept Bruno in motion, tipping his head, looking around, and talking to the audience. Then Oscar would pop out of his trash can and talk back to Bruno. I had a new character, and I also had a means of moving Oscar around without being seen.

Bruno was made of foam plastic, which eventually breaks down, and when he literally fell apart that was the end of him. He was a lot of fun to play. I had a pair of skates made for him so that I could roller-skate around the stage, with Oscar singing "I Love Trash!" Bruno's greatest moment was in the closing scene of *Follow That Bird,* as he slowly walks into the sunset carrying Oscar. Poor Bruno. I miss him.

10

GIVE IT A MONTH

The Balinese say that children walk with God.
That puts me in very good company.

—BIG BIRD

During my first year at *Sesame Street,* I found it impossible to make ends meet on my salary. Living in New York was expensive, and I still had to pay all the bills up at home in New England. And to make matters worse, when the taping season ended in April, Jim had no more work for me until *Sesame Street* began taping again in the fall.

Feeling desperate, I called my old friend Frank Avruch, Bozo the Clown, and he got me back on his show in Boston.

It was very strange to return to a commercial program after being on an educational show, especially one that was so good. It was a step backward, and I knew it. (Ever since then, I have had frequent dreams of having been called back into the military and serving overseas—somehow my mind sees a parallel in the two situations.) As much as I enjoyed working with Bozo, it was somewhat depressing to go back. Things were quite different on the set now, since budget cutbacks had caused them to eliminate the live audience. It was hard to create much excitement in a circus big top with no crowd—no cheering, no laughter, no lovely children excited to be on television.

Still, we had a lot of fun trying to make it interesting, doing plays with Bozo and my puppets, creating little musicals such as "Bozo, the Lost Prince of Bozalot."

When I had left *Bozo's Big Top* for *Sesame Street* the year before, the program director told me that I was making a big mistake and that I would never work in Boston again. Now that I was back, he offered me a chance to produce my own children's program. It would star Picklepuss, of course. I was sorely tempted. New York now seemed many leagues away.

Late summer came, and it was time to get ready for *Sesame*'s second season. I drove down to New York to be remeasured for the improved Big Bird puppet. I became very depressed about having to be there. New York was hot and filthy, and I wasn't sure where I would live for the season.

In spite of *Sesame Street*'s successes the first year, I was only offered a hundred-dollar weekly pay increase. In New York I would have to continue living like a student and be away from my home five days a week, while in Boston I'd have my own show and much better pay. As I walked up Broadway, I began to feel that the offer from Channel Five in Boston was far more appealing than anything in New York.

I decided that I'd have to bow out of *Sesame Street*. I took a bus to the East Side, over to Muppet headquarters.

I trudged up the stairs of the old carriage house with tears in my eyes, feeling very grave. I didn't know if I was doing the right thing, but I'd already made my decision. As I passed the workshop on the second floor, Kermit Love saw the look on my face and told me to wait.

"What's wrong?" he asked. I said that I just couldn't stay in New York. I had to go. I was going to tell Jim I was out.

"You really should not do this!" counseled Kermit. "You have an opportunity with this that you'll never get again. Don't blow it. At least stay one month, and then if you can't get with it, give Jim the word. Besides, you can't just abandon him like this. He needs you on the set come Monday. Give it one more month."

Kermit was right. *Sesame Street* was an opportunity that probably wouldn't come again. I shouldn't let Jim down. I would try one more month of playing Big Bird and Oscar. If I felt the same way at the end of that month, I would quit

and return to Boston. I walked back down the stairs and out the door.

About a week after I didn't quit the show, I spotted the latest *Time* magazine at a newsstand while bicycling to work. Big Bird's bright yellow head was beaming off the cover. I nearly fell off my bike. It suddenly seemed ridiculous that I had even considered leaving *Sesame Street*. I was getting more attention than I would ever get in Boston, and I was doing something really worthwhile at the same time. I realized that I had been one flight of stairs from forsaking my future.

By the middle of the second season, it was clear that *Sesame Street* was something really special. The people involved were dedicated and extremely creative, and the audience and the press loved the show. We were reaching kids through humor and good values, and the awards and outside appearances started to come in.

How could I have lost sight of a longtime dream come true? Being unhappy about being in New York was only a detail, and even though the pay was low, I hoped I'd overcome that too one day.

Sometimes you don't recognize that what you have is what you always wanted.

I t wasn't until I'd been playing Big Bird and Oscar for a few years that I came to understand what the characters really meant to people, especially children. There was a moment, an image really, that was more important to me than winning awards or appearing on magazine covers. It was a simple little drawing, but to me it symbolized everything I had hoped to achieve through puppets, television, and performing.

I was browsing around a little bookstore when I came upon a revolving rack of Little Golden Books. I picked one up to look at the illustrator's style, and when I was putting it away, I happened to notice the back cover. Surrounding a list of other Little Golden Books titles was a border fashioned from a curving musical staff. Dancing along with the musical notes were Minnie and Mickey Mouse, Donald and Daisy Duck, Snow White and Dopey, Bugs Bunny and Yosemite Sam—and Big Bird and Oscar.

There were *my* characters, perfectly cartooned, dancing with my favorite cartoon characters from childhood. This meant more to me than anything I had ever done, and it never would have happened if I'd stayed in Boston. "My God!" I said. "I've gotten up there with Bugs Bunny and Mickey Mouse!"

A warm glow flowed over me. What satisfaction I felt! Some of the most magical moments of my childhood were watching Disney cartoons. Seeing my characters dancing with Bugs and Mickey told me that I shared in those magic moments for other children. It hadn't hit me before. Now I knew that I had gotten to where I wanted to be.

11

WING IT

Don't be afraid to lay an egg.
—BIG BIRD

From early on, Big Bird and Oscar had lives that took them far away from *Sesame Street* and into the wider world of show business. When my characters started to make appearances on other shows and at events, I realized that they had become "personalities" that people, and not just children, found entertaining in their own right.

Each new appearance seemed to open another door and give me another opportunity to perform. I found that Big Bird and Oscar could hold their own with singers, dancers, comedians, actors, and talk-show hosts. I love working off the *Street*, meeting and collaborating with celebrities I admire. Often these appearances are unscripted, and I have to rely on the characters to come up with funny things to say. They almost always do. It seems the farther I take Big Bird and Oscar, the farther they take me.

n May 1970, the producers of the Emmys asked to have Big Bird be a guest presenter on the annual awards show, to be held in Carnegie Hall. When a Muppets producer phoned me about it I was thrilled.

Typical of many Emmy shows, it dragged quite a bit with too-long acceptance speeches and dull routines in between. Finally, it came time for my category. With a drumroll, Big Bird entered the hall from the back, running down the center aisle. I had him stop and greet a few individuals seated within reach. This was before I had a television monitor inside the puppet and I could barely see anything. I sat on an audience member's lap and later realized it was Cliff Robertson.

I was quite relieved to reach the stage without tripping over my Bird feet. Dick Cavett was waiting there to do our routine. The Bird couldn't remember his name and called him "Mr. Cabbage," "Mr. Cravat," and "Mr. Caveat." We got lots of laughs and then presented Burt Bacharach with his Emmy.

Backstage I found myself talking to Peter Ustinov, and being a huge fan and admirer of his incredible skills, I asked him to say something in his Indian accent. He responded in dialect and asked if he could put his head in Big Bird's mouth. Of course I agreed, and as we assumed the silly pose, fifty flashes went off. The picture on the front page of *The New York Times* the next morning was of Big Bird with Peter Ustinov's head in his mouth. The accompanying article said that Big

Bird and Dick Cavett provided the only lighthearted moment in an otherwise dull evening.

Apparently some Hollywood producers were watching, because soon I was invited to appear on a brand-new series, *The Flip Wilson Show*. At last I would get to work in Hollywood.

When rehearsals began in L.A., I found Flip to be very warm and fun to work with. The other guest stars were Raymond Burr, who, although intimidating at first, turned out to be a very sweet man, and James Brown, who was typically outrageous.

Sometime between the last rehearsal and the first taping of the show, they made a few changes to the set, including the addition of a low picket fence. I came out and took a step back, just as we'd rehearsed it, and tripped over the new fence. I never even saw it. I fell instantly into a seated position. My first concern was that the fragile head and beak would break, and

somehow, as I fell, I managed to hold the head and neck straight up. Big Bird subsequently looked very surprised as he landed, feet in the air, with a tremendous crash. A huge laugh came from the studio audience, and Raymond Burr gave me a hand and pulled me to my feet. We continued the scene from there and kept the take. The director was delighted. He told me it was the funniest entrance he'd seen since Martin and Lewis. I was just glad I didn't break the puppet.

One of the first talk shows I did as Oscar was with Dinah Shore. Once a guest's spot was finished, he stayed on the set, moving down one seat on a long couch that was next to Dinah. When I went on, Richard Dawson had just finished, so he was already sitting on the couch. There was a big throw pillow for me to put my arm behind, and Oscar appeared to be sitting between Dinah Shore and me. It was the simplest setup I had ever used.

I made a big mistake on that show. I thought it would be funny to make fun of Richard Dawson, who had long since moved on from *Hogan's Heroes* to *Family Feud.* Partway through Dinah's interview with Oscar, I had him say, "So, Dawson, how are things going over at *Hogan's Heroes?* Heh-heh!" It wasn't that funny. But worse, I gave him the floor. He took it and kept it. Dawson pulled out a long story, and by the time he was finished the time was up. Oscar never got to say another thing.

There were many variety shows and musicals on television in the seventies, and I got to do lots of Hollywood work. I was

teamed up with Susan Anton on an NBC musical special. We
sang a song about being tall: "How's the Weather up There?"
Another guest spot was with Cheryl Tiegs and John Ritter. I
got very annoyed with John, because he pulled a couple of the
Bird's feathers out as a joke.

In the mid-seventies my characters got booked onto
Hollywood Squares, which was then hosted by Peter Marshall.
Since then, I've been on more than 140 episodes and on every
version of the show.

The *Squares* is one of the most enjoyable programs on
which to guest. It's very lighthearted and silly, and a terrific
forum for ad-libbing. I find that Big Bird fits in better with the
humor on the show if I play him a little bit older, like a twelve-
year-old. He can be a little more flip and funny that way.

The set is made of angle iron and plywood, with an iron
spiral staircase on the right side. Each square is only about five
feet high, so the players have to lean over to get into their
square. Usually I'm assigned the square to the right of center so
that the elevated camera won't look down and see my head. I
sit right on the floor on a chair with the legs removed and hold
Big Bird's head up so he looks like he's sitting behind the desk.
There is a monitor under the desk so that I can see what's happening.

Since Big Bird is "sitting down" for the whole show, I only
need his left wing, head, and neck to give the illusion that he's
there. I work him like a regular puppet and don't even need to
take the body and legs with me to California.

Before each show is taped, the guests are given a list of general questions that they may be asked. For example, it might say that the first question is about whales and that "blubber" might make a good bluff answer. I find it hard to bluff every time, especially when I want one of the contestants to win. Helping the contestants isn't cheating on the *Squares,* because they have to decide whether to agree with you or not, based on their knowledge. When a housewife I was rooting for had forty-nine thousand dollars on the line, Big Bird assured her that he knew what he was talking about. She agreed with him and won the money.

One of many perks on the show is that at lunch all the stars sit together, so Deb and I have dined with the likes of Steve Martin, Dear Abby, Whoopi Goldberg, Roberta Peters, Richard Crenna, George Gobel, Gilbert Gottfried, Brad Garrett, Caroline Rhea, Doris Roberts, and the ever snarky Paul Lynde.

Rosie O'Donnell's show was fun to visit. Her on-air personality is jolly and enthusiastic, though I found that off-camera she is surprisingly subdued. One of my favorite visits on *Rosie* was with Oscar and Hillary Clinton. The First Lady brought Oscar some trash from the White House, including a couple of golf balls badly sliced by her husband. Oscar said that they looked like the president used an ax instead of a golf club.

One of the many times I've visited the *Today* show was when Big Bird appeared on his own postage stamp, in 1999.

The U.S. Postal Service had people vote on stamps they put out to commemorate each decade of the twentieth century. Big Bird was chosen as one of the stamps for the seventies. I felt honored. Big Bird was now an icon that represented a decade of American life.

When Katie Couric asked Big Bird how he felt about his stamp, I had him say, "You know, I'm really delighted to be on a stamp without having to die first."

In London I worked with royalty.

Oscar the Grouch and Prince Charles had a short skit to perform at the opening ceremony of the Museum of the Moving Image on the Thames, broadcast on the BBC. We used a prepared script, but the future king ad-libbed a little joke at the end of the piece. It was little enough that I regretfully can't remember it, though I will never forget working with a real prince.

I've performed in a number of places in Australia, New Zealand, Japan, the United Kingdom, Germany, and France. But Big Bird's farthest and most exciting trip away from Sesame Street came about because of a little joke I made in Hollywood to a great comedian.

12

MAKE 'EM LAUGH

> Hope is the thing with feathers.
> —EMILY DICKINSON

Debra and I were almost home one afternoon on our long ride from New York when we heard, "A Hollywood Minute. Here's Bob Hope," on the radio.

"What's up, Bob?" asked the host.

"I'm on my way to Beijing, Red China!" answered Mr. Hope.

"What are you going to do there?"

"I'm going to walk arm in arm down the main street of Beijing, Red China, with my old buddy, Big Bird!"

Deb and I looked at each other in disbelief. We were going to China. And we first heard about it on the news.

It had started three years earlier in Hollywood, in 1976. I'd been booked on a Bob Hope special and was very excited to

do a gig with one of America's most famous comedians. When I met Bob in his dressing room, it was obvious that he had never even heard of Big Bird. Bob's writers had requested Kermit the Frog, but he wasn't available because of Jim Henson's busy schedule. The Muppets offered Big Bird as an alternative. Gig Henry, one of Bob's writers, felt the Bird might work out, so I was booked. When I read the script, I found that the jokes they had written were mostly chicken and Colonel Sanders jokes, typical for Big Bird in Hollywood. I thought of something better.

When Bob Hope walked onto the stage for his warm-up, the Bird was waiting for him.

Bob saw the eight-foot yellow bird onstage and completely forgot what he was going to say. He pointed at the Bird and said, "Wow! Look at that!"

Big Bird looked at him and said, "I thought *I* had a funny-looking beak!"

Bob burst into great guffaws of laughter. He loves jokes about his nose—they're one of his trademarks—so I really got him with that. I followed up with "Gosh, I didn't know you'd be so short." He roared at that too.

He stepped close to the Bird and said, "Where are you in there, kid? Hey! Open with those lines! They're funnier than our stuff!"

My visit on his show was a big hit, and we went home in triumph.

After the show, he wrote me a simple letter that said: "Hey kid, you were very funny. You really made me laugh!" And he signed it, "Warmly, Bob Hope."

The whole thing had been a delightful experience, but I thought it was nothing more than a fun little moment in my Big Bird career. Little did I know that the joke about Bob Hope's nose would take me halfway around the world.

13

GO TO CHINA

 The humor of the Chinese people is seen in inventing gun-
powder and finding the best use in making fireworks
for their grandfathers' birthdays. —LIN YUTANG

When I was twelve, my best friend Ellen Day's mother
gave fifty thousand dollars to Dr. and Mrs. Saunders,
Methodist missionaries living in China. They used the money
to support their mission and to start a magazine in Nanking. I
became the magazine cartoonist, drawing "Lu Lee the Chinese
Dragon" for them until Mao chased them out of the country.
Working on my strips, I became quite fascinated with China.
I'd do research at my local library and try to imagine what it
was like on the other side of the world. Thanks to Bob Hope,
I would finally get to see China for myself.

Nixon had just visited China, and Bob had managed to
get permission to shoot the first western TV special there in
1979, with a little help from his friend Henry Kissinger. He
called it *On the Road to China,* like all his road movies with

Bing Crosby (*The Road to Bali* and so on). It was to be a three-hour variety show for NBC, and we were going all over China filming it. Bob's people put together an incredible bunch of performers, presenting the Chinese with a broad cross section of American culture—Crystal Gayle, mimes Shields and Yarnell, Mikhail Baryshnikov, who danced a soft-shoe number with Bob—it was a fun and talented group of people.

Peaches and Herb were also on the trip, but they turned out to be a poor selection as cultural ambassadors to China. They sang marvelously, but the problem was that their bit was to appear to make love to each other while singing. While they sang a very sensual song, she went down in front of him on her knees, facing him, and, well, the entire audience cringed and hid their eyes. It was complete culture shock, a pornographic show by Chinese standards.

My best performance on the tour was with Bob, which of course was a thrill in itself. We did a routine where Bob walked past a garden of tall canna plants, with their big, colorful flowers. Big Bird was hidden in the middle of them, and when Bob walked by I called to him, "Psst! Bob!"

He said, "Oh, it's you, Big Bird. What's the matter?"

I stage-whispered, "There've been four guys following me, dressed in white, with white hats, and they're licking their chops!"

Bob said, "Would they be cooks?"

"Yeah, that's what I'm worried about!"

"Don't worry, kid," he replied. "If you stick with me, you'll be safe!"

And we went into the Jule Styne / Stephen Sondheim song from *Gypsy:* "Wherever you go, whatever you do, we're gonna go through it together!" It was terrific.

China was even more incredible than I had imagined as a boy, and going with Bob Hope really was a privilege. He took a fancy to Deb, which was very much in our favor. Whenever the group was going anywhere, Bob would say, "Come on, darlin', you ride with me!" And they'd climb into one of those magnificent red-flag limousines made in Shanghai. They were based on a '55 Lincoln but were much bigger, and the only cars I've ever seen with hardwood floors.

Bob would sit like a king in the back, with his wife, Dolores, on one arm and Debra on the other. Then he'd see me standing outside the limousine and he'd say, "Well, I suppose you have to come too, huh, dummy?" I'd get in and sit on an enormous jump seat. It came so close to the backseat, Bob hardly had any room for his right knee. But he let me sit there anyway. He'd say, "You know, I must like you, kid. Because I never put up with any discomfort at all. I like to live like a king!"

Everybody else was riding around in a big Toyota bus, while we sat in Bob's red-flag limo and got to listen to him comment on everything we saw and tell us stories from his life. Every time we went anywhere it was a real joy, because Bob was absolutely hilarious. He was nothing like the Bob Hope you see on TV with his corny jokes and his cue cards. He's a hundred times funnier in person. When he's not working off a script, he tells the most interesting and hysterical stories.

There was a funny thing about being the first western entertainers in China: people had no idea who we were. When we first arrived, Bob had already been there for a week. His daughter Linda, who was a producer on the show, came to our room in the Beijing hotel and said, "Bob would like to greet you." Then she told us, "He's kind of unhappy, because nobody's ever heard of him in China!" He really likes recognition. So we went up to his room and he said, "Howya doing, kid?" He calls everybody kid.

I said, "They tell me that nobody's heard of you here. Isn't that kind of a relief to have some privacy for a change?"

"Are you kidding?" he said. "I'm miserable! Nobody knows who I am!"

In China it's a real struggle for many people just to live, even now, but it was particularly so then. The average person made something like twenty-seven dollars a year, and there was very little fantasy and delight in life. Imagine what it must have been like to suddenly see a giant yellow bird walking down the street. When they saw Big Bird for the first time, they had no idea who he was or what he was doing there. It didn't matter. They were so happy to see this fantastic thing come into their lives that they smiled with pure joy. Big Bird's personality was perfectly suited to the situation. He's so open to making friends, he's kind and he's gentle, and he's very approachable. It was easy for me to find ways of getting Big Bird to interact with people as we traveled the country.

One of the segments of the special was a Chinese puppet show. Big Bird went to the Shanghai Puppet Theater to tape a presentation of "The Monkey King Defeats the White Bone Demon." Big Bird sat in the first row of an audience full of Chinese children, and periodically throughout the performance, the director cut to Big Bird's reactions to the show. This was actually a difficult assignment for me, because the performance was forty-five minutes long, which is a very long time to hold the Bird's head aloft. I was also frustrated because I could barely see the show through the peephole between feathers. From what I could see, however, the performance was excellent.

After the story ended, Big Bird took the stage. An interpreter explained to the audience that we were going to sing a song together. Big Bird would sing something, and when he pointed his wing at them, they should sing the same thing back. The song I sang was "Sing What I Sing," by Tony Geiss, and it's one of the best audience-participation songs I know.

It's in English of course, but the words to repeat are just non-sense sounds, so I thought it would be able to bridge the language barrier.

When I started to sing, I could see that all attention was on the giant yellow bird in the front of the hall. I sang "Tra-la-la," and pointed. The children sang "Tra-la-la," and I knew I had them. In the middle of the song, I had them sing "Fiddle-diddle-dee," more and more quietly, until Big Bird started to fall asleep. I got a laugh for that, and then a bigger laugh when Big Bird started to snore. I had him wake up and finish the song. The idea worked perfectly. I managed to entertain and engage with an audience of children who couldn't understand a word I said.

Everywhere I went, I found the Chinese people to be extremely down-to-earth and to have a sense of humor similar to that of Americans. It was a great pleasure to get out into the streets and the countryside and bring Big Bird to the real China. I found it easy to connect with people through physical humor, like having Big Bird hunt for a flea in his feathers with his beak and then suddenly sneeze. I loved meeting the people both in costume and as myself.

The people were what made me want to go back so badly. The government there was, as a whole, rather cold and unyielding to human desires, yet the people were honest and open. We would be out shopping, just walking around, and people would come up to us and ask where we were from. We would tell them and they would welcome us to China with genuine warmth. In one store, we got applause from everyone there just for walking in the door.

The government officials that I encountered, however, would use what little power they had to inconvenience people. But even our translator, who was also a spy, was very friendly when he told us that he was making reports on us. I found out about this when he was yawning and falling asleep at breakfast one day. I asked him why he was so tired. We had all gone to bed early the night before.

"Not me," he said, "I was up until two in the morning writing my report on you. I have to write down everything you say every day and send it to my superior."

"You write down everything we say?" I asked.

"Yes," he said.

In a loud voice I cried, "China is the most wonderful country I've ever visited! I love everything about it, especially the government!"

The trip was over far too soon. It had all happened so fast, I had barely taken it in before it was time to go home. I had finally gotten to go to places I had only read about—the Great Wall, Tiananmen Square, the Forbidden City, Shanghai—but I had barely seen anything at all. We were working almost the entire time, and as I've said, when I'm in costume I literally can't see much of anything. We were also constantly moving from location to location, and China is a very big place.

Even before we left, Debra and I were working on a plan to return. The way people, especially children, reacted to Big Bird was so warm, strong, and positive that we knew that he should come back. There was a real need for him there, and we were determined to find a way to bring him back.

14

WRITE YOUR OWN STORY

> I love being a writer.
> What I can't stand is the paperwork.
> —PORFIRIO DIAZ

esame Street has always been about social values as much as it has been about learning the alphabet, and it has been recognized for becoming a very positive part of American culture. I thought that if *Sesame Street* could go to China, we could do something that would help bring Chinese culture and social values back to China a little bit, as well as to show China's warm and friendly side to the rest of the world.

The tour with Bob Hope had been lots of fun, but it was really just an entertaining variety show that used the various locations we visited as backdrops for our skits. We poked around the country in a superficial way and put on our show wherever we happened to be. With *Sesame Street,* I thought that we could do something in story form, integrating Chinese places, tales, and people into the plot. Most of all, I wanted Big Bird to interact more with the children; they had been so fascinated with him on the first trip, so curious, smart, and adorable. The children were the only people in China wearing bright colors; adults all wore olive drab or navy blue Mao suits at the time. Often, in the villages we'd pass, the children's vibrant reds, yellows, and greens provided the only contrast against a monotone beige world.

Debra and I worked on a story outline that went like this: Big Bird would discover that he was related to the Phoenix and decide to go to China to find her. Along the way, he would meet the Monkey King, who's sort of the Chinese Bugs Bunny, very mischievous and magical, and he'd also get help from a child who would accompany him on his journey. It was a simple idea that naturally flowed from things we had learned during our first experience in China.

We presented the idea to the *Sesame Street* producers, and amazingly, they approved it. They assigned the project to Jon Stone. From the start, I had mixed feelings about their choice. On the one hand, Jon was a terrific director. Having been a writer, he was excellent at adapting a script once shooting had begun, and he was also very good at incorporating my ad-libs into a scene. On the other hand, for some reason that I've never been sure of, he went through periods of not liking me at all. So, while I knew the choice of Jon Stone would make it a difficult trip, I also knew that it would result in a very good show.

At a lunch meeting to discuss the project, Jon confessed that he had never paid much attention to China and knew next to nothing about it. Debra and I bought some books to show him some of the locations that we had scouted on the first trip, and especially Guilin, which we hadn't visited but knew would be perfect for this story. Using this material and the outline that we had drawn up, Jon put together the story of Big Bird's quest to find the Phoenix. He had it start out in New York's Chinatown, where Big Bird sees a picture of the Phoenix and gets some other clues before setting off for China to find her. He also added Barkley the dog, played by Brian Meehl, to the story. Jon wrote an excellent script, and three years after the trip with Bob Hope, we were off to China again, to tape *Big Bird in China,* also for NBC.

Just as I had feared, it turned out to be a very difficult trip for me, mainly because of Jon Stone's animosity. He made me feel like he was the teacher and I was the kid in class who could never get the answer right. I was back in school again, being bullied, and I was miserable. One would never guess that I was the star of this minimovie. Jon was angry with me the whole time, and to this day I don't know why.

Despite the tension, Jon and I still worked well together. There were endless unforeseen problems and details to iron out that just couldn't be predicted from New York, and the whole group really pulled together as an ensemble to solve them. But once the cameras stopped rolling, he didn't want to have anything to do with me.

One wonderful thing that happened was meeting Lien Tsu, the little girl who had been picked to play Xiao Fu, or Little

Lotus, who helps Big Bird find the Phoenix. (She told the Chinese producers that she was six, but she was really only five.) Lien Tsu was enchantingly beautiful and very, very smart. The moment we saw her, Debra and I fell madly in love with her.

Lien Tsu didn't speak any English when we started, but we never had a communication problem; we just used gestures and expressions, and she understood everything. Jon would give her complicated directions in English, telling her where to be in a shot or how to walk from one place to another and stay on camera. We'd walk through a scene and then she'd get it, every time.

It was on this trip that I finally got to see Guilin. No picture does it justice—it is truly one of the most beautiful places on earth. Guilin is an old city, surrounded by mountains that look like green baguettes standing on end. The Li River runs through the city, and the mountains come right down to its banks. The scene we shot there was one of my favorites in the show. It was also the most dangerous.

In the script it seemed very simple—a shot of Big Bird, Barkley the dog, and Xiao Fu going downstream on a little boat. What made it life-threatening were the monsoon rains in the mountains that were flooding the river so that it rose about a foot every five minutes.

We got on the boat, which had a hut in the middle for the costume handler and the boat driver. The dog, the little girl, and I were on the bow, looking downstream. The driver

pushed off and we were swept into the swirling river. It wouldn't take much to tip over; one big wave or a sudden shifting of weight, and I'm sure we would have sunk. Between the costumes, my big feet, and the stilts clamped to Brian's arms, there was a good chance that we would drown if we did. Lien Tsu couldn't swim and was so small she would have been swept away before anyone could get to her. It was very frightening but quite majestic, rushing down the river with the beautiful mountains all around us. We were carried downstream for about a half mile, until the handler's walkie-talkie crackled and Jon said that he had the shot. The driver held the boat in place with a quivering pole while a motorboat came to bring us back to the tour ship we used as a camera platform. Debra greeted us with hugs, thankful to have us all safely back.

When it was time to go, we all went to the airport together, where Debra and I were to catch our plane to Hong Kong. We had over an hour before our flight, and Debra and I were on line to go through customs when we saw some officials take Lien Tsu and her mother away somewhere. We had to stay where we were as we watched them go, without having said good-bye. It was unbearably sad and gave us a hint of the powerlessness average Chinese people must have felt in relation to their state. Stone-faced officials kept us moving through customs while others held Lien Tsu and her mother in a room in another part of the airport for no other reason than to keep us apart, to keep us from saying good-bye as friends would do. It was awful.

The time ticked away and we were in another line, about to board the plane, when suddenly we heard Lien Tsu call our names. The officials had let her and her mother out of the room so that they could say good-bye to us with only two minutes to spare. A huge crowd of people separated us. Lien Tsu's mother picked her up, and the people passed her to one another over their heads until she reached us and fell into our arms. We were all crying, and she said "I luff you" while we said *"Wo ai ni,"* and we hugged and hugged. Then we passed her back to her mother, got on the plane, and never saw her again.

ig Bird in China was a hit, in both the United States and China. China had the rights to show it as much as they wanted, and in the years after we made it, it aired many times on television. I was glad that it was successful, but there was something else about the experience that I knew was very important for Big Bird and for me. I had seen China change a little bit in the three years since my first visit. Things were a little more open, and people seemed just a little more free. Before the first trip we would not have been allowed to film *Big Bird in China.* I hoped that, in whatever small way, Big Bird had helped to make life there a little happier and to make the children a little more hopeful. However it had happened, Big Bird played a tiny part in this very exciting chapter of China's history, and I hoped he would continue to have a role in it. At the very least, I wanted to go back when I wasn't working.

15

PRETEND YOU CAN DANCE

How inimitably graceful children are
in general before they learn to dance.
—SAMUEL TAYLOR COLERIDGE

I am a terrible dancer. I have no ability to move my feet in time and remember where I'm supposed to put them. I cannot sing, count 1-2-3-4 in my head, and remember the moves I'm supposed to make. And that's when I'm *not* inside a puppet. When I'm in a puppet, I'm awful. Or at least I was, until I got some good advice from a friend.

Big Bird is always being asked to dance. When he'd get booked on variety shows or one of the Muppet specials, inevitably they'd write a song-and-dance number for him. Once I got so frustrated trying to learn a routine I actually cried because I could see the disappointment on Jim Henson's face. I whined to him, "Why do you always put me in dance numbers? I just can't dance!"

He thought about it and answered, "Because Big Bird is the only Muppet with legs!"

When I appeared on *The Flip Wilson Show* in 1970, we had a choreographer who had planned an elaborate dance routine for Big Bird and Flip. His name was Jack.

I struggled to learn the steps Jack had shown me, but by the end of each attempt he would be shaking his head and burying his face in his hands. I was determined to get the dance right, if for no other reason than to lift Jack's depression. At last I did every move correctly and with style. Jack was beaming. Then the director said that they'd have to shoot it one more time, and we taped it again. Afterward, Jack was back to shaking his head. That was the take that aired.

In 1977 I guested on *Donny and Marie*. When I saw that I was to be in a big dance scene, I expressed my concern. They said not to worry, the choreographer would show me what to do. He sure did. He demonstrated a dance worthy of Gene Kelly and said, "Now you do it!"

I couldn't. They had to radically simplify my moves to basic steps. In the end it all came out fine, since Donny and Marie are very talented. They were the ones who shone in that scene. No one noticed that I just followed them around clomping in my big, wide Bird feet.

When I was a guest on *The Muppet Show,* I was teamed up with Leslie Uggams for a big dance number. Paddy Stone, the legendary choreographer, showed me what they expected, and I was apprehensive. I tried over and over to do the turns and moves, but I couldn't get near the dance he had worked out.

Then Jim suggested that one of the Paddy Stone dancers get in the puppet to do the segment that required the dance moves. The dancer got in the suit and the Bird's feet did exactly the right steps—but his head hung to one side, and he appeared to be in a coma. Like dancing, puppetry isn't learned overnight. The dancer couldn't put a modicum of life in the Bird's head and facial expressions.

I ended up doing the Bird in the dance scene, using some simple steps I could manage while Leslie beautifully danced her heart out. It was a sweet scene, but I wished that I could actually dance. Then I'd be able to enjoy the performance and make it look a lot better too.

Richard Hunt, another Muppeteer, heard my complaint and made an insightful suggestion.

"Forget about what those people are telling you to do," he advised. "Just have Big Bird think he's a good dancer—the best dancer in the world. *Pretend* he can dance."

I hadn't put myself in that mode before. Maybe if the Bird believed he could dance, he'd have the confidence I lacked. Big Bird's personality is so well developed and so strong that *he* can influence *me*. I can feel what he is thinking and feeling and draw on that as I perform. If he thought he could dance, he might carry me through the performance.

I tried it right away. I did a special for PBS that featured Isaac Stern playing his Stradivarius, prima ballerina Cynthia Gregory, and Big Bird.

I reminded myself that Big Bird thinks he can dance beautifully, and we launched into our routine. Around and around we whirled, and the Bird had a wonderful time, dipping and twirling his partner across the shiny floor. It was a success, and instead of being miserable, I actually had fun.

Later Big Bird was booked on the *Night of 100 Stars* at Radio City Music Hall. I was delighted to appear with the likes of Jimmy Stewart, Katharine Hepburn, Douglas Fairbanks, Jr., Muhammad Ali, and Laurence Olivier. Stepping onto that huge stage with all of those talented people was an awesome feeling. Big Bird was to be in a song-and-dance number with the Rockettes, the most precise dancers in the world. Would pretending Big Bird could dance work at Radio City?

I came out onstage and sang a short song. Then came the dance, a strutting soft-shoe number with a straw hat and cane. My own personal Rockette, Mary Sixx Rupert, who possessed the most perfect legs I have ever seen, started dancing with Big Bird. Keeping Richard's advice in mind, I told myself that Big Bird was a terrific dancer. Big Bird got so carried away that he wouldn't stop dancing, and Mary Sixx had to dance him offstage by pushing him to the wings. It was the best dance number I've ever done, and it worked because Big Bird believed that he could do it and I believed in him.

16

HEAR THE MUSIC

When words leave off, music begins.
—ARTHUR HELPS

In June 1971 *Sesame Street* was invited to make a television special with the Boston Pops, conducted by Arthur Fiedler. The whole cast was involved in the production, and I got to conduct the symphony as the Bird.

In rehearsal, Mr. Fiedler handed me his baton and said, "Go ahead." The orchestra was going to play a simple chord. I was very intimidated, having had no musical training, and I told him I had no idea what I should do. He then gave me the only lesson in conducting I ever got.

"Raise the baton," he said. "Then bring it down, and they will play."

I stepped up on the conductor's platform. Using my left hand, since my right is always in the Bird's head, I tapped the music stand for the orchestra's attention, then raised the baton and brought it down. A mighty chord came back at me from all eighty instruments in the orchestra. It was so startling I almost dropped the baton.

For the first time, I realized what power a conductor has. I had a fantastic time doing the skit, and the program was a success.

Kermit Love thought that we could build a whole concert series around Big Bird conducting and doing musical bits as a child's introduction to the orchestra. With the help of *Sesame*'s music director, Dave Conner, we built a seventy-minute program that had Big Bird conducting, singing, roller-skating, and playing the toy piano. I believe that it was one of the best introductions to the orchestra available for young children. We had kids as young as two and three coming to Symphony Hall and enjoying the performance.

Our first show was in Hawaii. Kermit's friend Joseph Levine was conductor for the Honolulu Symphony, and he agreed to have the orchestra present the show.

The first song in the program was "Somebody Come and Play." Here I made a mistake. On a musical bridge in the middle of the song, I had the Bird plaintively say, "Won't someone come and play with me?" Chaos! Children ran down the aisle, and about twenty-eight of them managed to climb up onstage and surround Big Bird. I was relieved that not one child attempted to pull a feather. After the song, the kids went back to their seats and I made a mental note not to say that again.

That was the beginning of a series of symphony concerts that lasted eight years. I conducted orchestras from coast to coast and in Canada and Australia. For five years I conducted the Vancouver Symphony Orchestra working with Richard Hayman, a delightful man who had arranged Leroy Anderson's songs, such as "Sleigh Ride" and "The Typewriter." Big Bird, using his mixed-up-name bit from *Sesame,* called Richard "Mr. Haystack" and "Mr. Hayface."

The Australian Broadcasting Company invited me to conduct the Melbourne Symphony on a riverboat as part of the city's annual Moomba Days celebration. I was told that the audience was over 300,000 people spread out on both sides of the Yarra River. The boat was parked so the 220,000 people on the city side of the river would be favored with the best view. We did the whole show for them, and when we finished, the 80,000 people behind us began to chant, "What about us? What about us?"

Since 80,000 was the second-largest audience I've ever had, I agreed to do the show again and we turned the boat to face the other bank of the river. It was exhausting, but that many people should not be denied.

I learned a lot about music by conducting some of the

finest orchestras in the world. One of the things I discovered was that some pieces were entirely inappropriate for very young children. The Buffalo Symphony chose to play Stravinsky's *The Firebird* on the strength of the title alone—I guess they thought the bird theme would go well with Big Bird. As soon as they began the piece, I noticed that it sounds a lot like the music that plays when the shark is approaching in *Jaws.* The kids were terribly frightened and upset.

Saint-Saëns's *Carnival of the Animals* was another piece chosen for its title. The piece included lots of effete narration written by Ogden Nash, and it proved to be very boring for the young audience. I don't think anybody understood the too-clever poems, and the music itself was interminable. I could sense the kids' restless discomfort as I spoke, and when I thought about having to do the show all over again later in the day, I decided to cut that piece from the routine in the future.

When the children are running up and down the aisles until something better begins, it's a clear sign that a bad choice has been made. A good piece is instantly obvious when half the kids begin "conducting" themselves, with little waving arms.

We found the *William Tell* Overture was a big hit. Kids loved the drama and "galloping" excitement of the music. Another success was the "Moonlight Medley" that Dave Conner put together. First, I conducted part of the *Moonlight* Sonata. Then I sang portions of "Moonlight and Roses," "On Moonlight Bay," and "Blue Moon."

Perhaps my favorite part of the concert was when Oscar

sang "I Love Trash" with a full orchestra behind him. There was such a contrast between his grouchy voice and lyrics and the beautiful sound of a symphony orchestra playing the melody. The audience loved it.

There were downsides to doing so many shows. It seemed Deb and I could never unpack because we were always leaving home for another performance. Worse, the performances entailed extreme discomfort for me. I would make five appearances in the hour-and-ten-minute shows, with only a few minutes in between. The orchestra would play while I was off-stage, and the kids in the audience would become impatient for the music to end and Big Bird to come back. Meanwhile, those "breaks" were intense. My right arm would be aching from holding up the almost five pounds of the Bird's head, and I would be covered with sweat. I had to take off the Bird, remove my two wireless mikes, change my T-shirt, and breathe oxygen through a mask to have the energy to go out again for another grueling routine. I would just manage to get everything back on, and off I went again. If I was switching to Bruno the trash man, I had to change everything and then change it all back again for the Bird's next act. I would lose three to four pounds during a show, and afterward, my face would be as gray as my hair.

After eight years I grew weary of management problems, touring, and sweating so much and decided to end my concert series. My last performance was at the Blossom Center near Cleveland, conducting the Cleveland Orchestra. It was a won-

derful show in a beautiful place, and it was with a lot of nos-
talgia that I peeled off my soaking-wet T-shirt at the end of the
show. I'd been to many cities all over the land, and for the final
appearance I got to conduct an orchestra that is considered
one of the greatest in the world, second only to the London
Symphony. Not a bad way to finish that phase of my career.

17

WATCH YOUR STEP

Bravery is the capacity to perform properly
even when scared half to death.
—OMAR BRADLEY

There are many jobs that are inherently hazardous—
meatpacker, firefighter, lion tamer—but most people
probably don't think of puppeteering that way. I didn't either,
but I discovered that it could be very dangerous indeed.

In the first season of *Sesame Street,* I was standing in front
of Hooper's in costume, ready to do a scene, when a two-
thousand-watt klieg light crashed to the floor two feet away.
The lamp was huge, burning hot, and weighed at least a hundred pounds, so I was relieved that it missed me and I was still
alive. Then I smelled smoke. I looked down inside the Bird
suit and saw flames.

Some burning asbestos chunks had flown out in the crash
and set fire to my left Bird leg. I tried to get out of the suit, but
the puppet was strapped to me tightly. Unable to take it off on

my own, I began to fear I would burn to death. Bravely, a cameraman named Richie King clapped the flames out with his bare hands. When the smoke cleared, a large portion of the lower cloth legging was completely burned away. It turns out the cloth was highly flammable and my skin had been protected only by the tall leather boots I wore beneath the costume at that time.

Only two weeks later there was another incident. We were set up to shoot a scene that called for Oscar to produce lots of black smoke from a smoke factory inside his trash can. Since standard smoke machines produce only white smoke, one of the electricians decided he would have to burn rubber to create black smoke for the bit.

Behind the trash can he had erected a small shelf that held a pie pan filled with kerosene and bits of black rubber. I had to duck under the arrangement to get in position to have Oscar pop up at the right time. I told the electrician I didn't like the setup, that it looked downright dangerous to have it burning right above my head.

"Don't worry about it," he assured me as he put a match in the liquid. Blue flames danced around the rubber, and black smoke began to curl upward.

"Countdown to action—five, four . . . ," came the call. The oil began to boil. The electrician lowered a stovepipe over the flaming liquid, and as a roar erupted, I stood up and pushed the whole trash-can unit forward so I could escape this frightening inferno.

"Hey! Get back in there!" the floor manager shouted. "We're rolling!"

"Not me!" I replied. At that instant the stovepipe exploded and the flames burst fifteen feet up the side of the brownstone. Panic took over as people frantically searched for fire extinguishers. There didn't seem to be any on the set floor. Some were brought in from outside, and the fire was put out. The inside of the trash can was totally burned out, exactly where my head would have been.

Later we did the scene again with cool white smoke and without the electrician.

I did a lot of stage appearances in the seventies and eighties where the hazards were more apparent. I often had to work on temporary portable stages of varying heights, and these could be treacherous indeed.

In Baltimore, I accidentally stepped off the stage, dropped three feet to the floor, and landed on my knees. I jumped up and had the Bird say, "Boy, that first step is a doozy!"

In another auditorium, our temporary stage was seven feet above the floor. There were no rails to keep one from falling off, so a man was stationed to the side, to stop me from going too far and falling over the edge.

I did my performance and then, after waving good-bye, ran off into the wings. The guard just clapped and let me run on past him, right toward the edge. Debra saw it all and ran after me. "You were supposed to stop him!" she shout-whispered to the guard. At that moment I felt my foot go off the edge—I was beginning to fall. Deb had to push up the bottom hoop of the Bird's body and grab my belt, the only solid way to hold on to me. I was already starting to go forward, and she threw herself backward to try to pull me back from the abyss. She hit the floor and I landed on her lap. This happened in the dark, and moments later when all the lights came up we looked down to where I would have landed seven feet below. There were dozens of chairs stored there, with a forest of pointed chrome legs jutting upward. Big Bird would have been impaled.

A few years back, the producers decided to put some rappers on the program. They found a trio of young men to do some scenes with Big Bird. One of the bits written for them was to rap the alphabet. The lead rapper chanted, "A to the B, to the C, to the D, E, F . . ." Unfortunately, he had to do the scene three times because he kept leaving out some of the alphabet. On the fourth try he got it right, but then I blew the closing line. When he was told he'd have to do it one more time, he lost his cool. He yelled, "Stupid bird," and then hit Big Bird across the beak so hard he knocked the head right out of my hand. Big Bird's head dangled straight down, as if his neck had been broken. Everyone gasped, and I worried that the punch might have broken the fragile beak. Big Bird survived the blow, but I never saw that rapper on the show again.

18

BE PERSISTENT

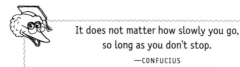

It does not matter how slowly you go,
so long as you don't stop.
—CONFUCIUS

When I was coming up on my fifteenth year of working for the Muppets, Richard Hunt suggested to Jim that he honor the occasion with a party. This was pretty unusual. I can't remember another party at Muppets being given for something like that and I never got another one, but Jim liked Richard's idea. He threw a big party for me, and boy, could Jim throw a party.

It was held at the Muppet Mansion, a beautiful East Side townhouse that had been a lovely home years ago and was now decorated in whimsical Muppet style, with props and creatures in every nook and cranny, contraptions hanging from the ceiling, and fantastic paintings on the walls.

The conference room was the center of the party, and a pianist at the grand piano provided the music. Jim never scrimped when he entertained, and there was caviar and hors d'oeuvres and lots of champagne.

Jim gave me a gold pocket watch and asked me to say a few words.

The first thing I said was, "Well, I got my gold watch. Does this mean I'm being retired?" This got a laugh. Then I looked at the engraved watch and saw that it was a Waltham. I said, "I don't know if you know this, but my father spent most of his life working at the Waltham watch factory. He probably made the screws that are in this gorgeous timepiece."

It's ironic that if Dad had convinced me to work at Waltham, I might have helped make a watch like this, instead of being given one for performing puppets, as I had always wanted to do.

Then I said, "I want to thank you: for the watch, and for fifteen wonderful years with the Muppets. I want to say that becoming Big Bird is the *second* greatest thing that has ever happened to me," and I put my arm around Debi, who was standing right next to me. Everybody knew what the greatest thing that had ever happened to me was.

You might think that because I'm an artist, I would be very good at recognizing faces. Not so.

The first time I saw Debra she was sitting at her desk at the Children's Television Workshop. I screwed up my courage, walked right over to her, and introduced myself. She smiled at me, and I asked her if she would like to go out to dinner with me after work. My heart sank when she told me that she was expected at home to cook dinner for her husband. As I walked away, I wasn't really surprised. Of course she'd be taken. She was so cute, with an adorable pixie hairdo.

A half year later, at the CTW Christmas party at the Tavern on the Green, I spotted a lovely young lady with a Dutch-boy haircut across the room. I went over to her and she smiled at me. After chatting a little bit, I asked her if she'd like to sit with me for dinner. Disappointment crept in when she informed me that she had to leave the party to go home to her husband. Once again I thought to myself, Too bad the girls I feel attracted to are already spoken for.

Months went by, and I went to a recording studio in New York City to record an album for *Sesame Street*. I was approached by a pretty girl with the most beautiful smile and lovely brown hair that touched her collar and we immediately hit it off. She seemed to know me, though I didn't know how. She told me that since her marriage had recently ended, she was living with her family on Long Island. I was about to go on tour for the show, but I promised to call her when I got back.

Three months later I met her at the office building that houses the Children's Television Workshop in Lincoln Square and we walked toward Central Park. We held hands as we crossed Central Park West on our way to the Tavern on the Green.

Before we finished dinner, we both knew in our hearts that

we would be married. It really was love at first sight. Thirteen days after our first date, we were walking down Broadway when, at Sixty-second Street, I was completely overpowered with the most complete, fantastic, wonderful feeling. I stopped and blurted out, "You will marry me, won't you?" And she said, "Y-y-y-yes." I spun her around and kissed her. I was already more in love than I'd ever been in my life. It's been that way ever since. In almost thirty years, there's never been a moment when I felt that we'd been too hasty. I could have proposed the first night—almost two weeks was too long a wait.

A few months after my proposal we were in Zurich, Switzerland, enjoying the all-expenses-paid trip that Debra had won on a TV quiz show. At dinner she raised her wineglass to me and said, "Here's to your persistence. Thank you for never giving up on me."

I was puzzled. "What do you mean?" When she described the three times I had asked her out I exclaimed, "You mean, you were all those girls?" Her hair had grown between the first time I asked her out and the third. It's a good thing I didn't recognize her each time. If I had, I would never have approached her again, after finding out that she was married.

Debra and I have such a fantastic relationship, I'm afraid we sometimes ignore other people. As nice as it can be visiting with friends, it's not as nice as spending an evening alone together. We've adopted the motto "There's no time to lose" and apply it to each day of our marriage. Knowing what it's like to be with her, I don't want to waste a day that we could be together, enjoying life. That, I think, speaks of a really terrific marriage.

19

EAT YOUR VEGGIES

Food is an important part of a balanced diet.
—FRAN LEBOWITZ

One place I never expected puppets to take me was the White House. Television, Hollywood, Europe, even China seemed like more plausible venues for performing the big, yellow bird. But Big Bird must be a bit of a diplomat, for he's allowed me to meet six First Ladies.

At *Sesame Street* we were thrilled in 1971 when Pat Nixon asked us to appear at the White House's annual Christmas party for the children of diplomats from around the world. Joe Raposo directed the program, which took place in the East Wing. We performed songs and skits, and all the kids were dressed in traditional costume from their homelands. It was a lovely party.

At the end of the performance, Mrs. Nixon stepped up onto our platform for a photo session. Often when I pose with people, I put the Bird's left wing around their shoulders. It makes a nice picture, with the person being half buried in feathers. I thought that putting my wing around the First Lady might be too informal, so I merely put my hand on her right shoulder. She immediately reached up and took my hand down, and held it there until all the pictures were snapped. I made a mental note: don't put your wing on the First Lady.

It must not have been too bad a faux pas, for she sent me a lovely framed picture of her and Big Bird and an autographed book of President Nixon's memoirs. Mrs. Nixon was a gracious host.

The next First Lady, Betty Ford, had a different attitude about getting close to Big Bird and hugged the puppet with both arms after another Christmas performance at the White House.

Deb and I accidentally caused a security incident at that party. I had finished performing and was in my dressing area, which was in a small dining room. Deb went out into the hall and asked Mrs. Ford if she wanted to pose for a picture with Big Bird. Mrs. Ford agreed and left the hall so quickly to come inside the dining room, the Secret Service wasn't sure where she'd gone. We took the picture and spent a few minutes chatting with the First Lady. Then the door flew open, and the Secret Service agents came hurrying in, extremely agitated. They had actually lost the First Lady for five minutes right in the White House.

Rosalynn Carter, as Mrs. Ford had done, continued the Christmas-party tradition. She was quiet and shy but very sweet. Our visit with her was brief but long enough to get a picture taken of her and the Bird.

My next White House invitation came from Mrs. Reagan for an Easter performance on the grounds. It was a big stage show starring cast members of Broadway's *Barnum* and *Annie,* my old friend Hervé Villechaize, and Big Bird.

In the middle of the show there was some kind of scheduling mix-up. The kids from *Barnum* were singing and dancing, and the crowd of five thousand parents and children were enjoying the performance. Suddenly an announcement over the loudspeakers told everyone to report to the Truman Balcony, on the other side of the lawn, to be greeted by the First Lady.

Our show stopped and the crowd walked slowly away, gathered up at the White House, and waited for the First Lady to appear.

She stepped out and waved to the crowd. Then she went back inside.

On the other side of the lawn, I was asked to begin my Big Bird performance.

"But there's no one here," I protested.

"They'll be here shortly. You'd better start singing," I was advised.

I began singing "Somebody Come and Play" to an empty lawn. The South Lawn has a huge rolling hill rising toward the back, and as I sang, five thousand people answered Big Bird's call. They came over the crest, like the cavalry arriving in a Hollywood western. Many of the children were on their fathers' shoulders, all rushing to the front for a good view. It was an awesome sight.

By far the most jolly and gregarious of the First Ladies I have met is Barbara Bush. I did a series of storytelling tapes with her for her Children's Literacy Program, and later she invited Debra and me to the White House for tea. She was absolutely charming and very outgoing. At Christmastime she also had Big Bird perform in the East Wing for the annual children's party.

In 1992 I was invited to a dinner in Dallas honoring Ralph Rogers, who created PBS. I did a routine as the Bird and presented an award to Mr. Rogers. Then I got into my tuxedo, and Debra and I were invited to sit with George W. Bush and his wife, Laura. This was while he owned the Texas Rangers baseball team, before he was governor or president. After a pleasant dinner, everyone was asked to go into the lobby to greet Barbara Bush. As she arrived, her eyes locked on mine, and she brushed past a line of dignitaries saying, "Excuse me, everyone, I have to greet an old friend." To my surprise, she came right to me and put her arms around me.

"How's my dear birdie friend?" she asked.

"I think I'm in love!" I replied.

When she broke her leg sledding with her grandchildren at Camp David, I sent her a card that opened to a picture of Big Bird with his wing in a sling. It read, "Sorry to hear about your accident. One time I broke my wing, and I am sorry to hear that you broke your drumstick." Her reply said, "Thank you for the card you drew for me. Drumstick, eh? Well, maybe you're right. Your friend, Barbara Bush."

I've had the honor of working with Hillary Clinton on a number of occasions. When Bill Clinton was first in office, Mrs. Clinton had some of the *Sesame Street* characters perform in the Rose Garden. While we were setting up, she sat on the rug in the China Room and played with some of the puppets we had brought. She had a great sense of humor, and it was a pleasant time.

When she later put in an appearance on *Sesame Street* there was a bit of a brouhaha. During the previous administration, President Bush had gotten into trouble for telling the country that he didn't have to eat his broccoli. Mrs. Clinton was doing a bit on our show to promote "eating your veggies." When the list of vegetables was too long for the allotted time, cuts had to be made. Mrs. Clinton suggested cutting peas and said that nobody liked them anyway. A reporter from the *New York Post* had sneaked onto the set, and the following day's headline read: PLEASE, MRS. CLINTON, GIVE PEAS A CHANCE.

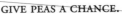

20

BE HONEST WITH YOUR AUDIENCE

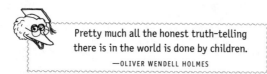

Pretty much all the honest truth-telling
there is in the world is done by children.
—OLIVER WENDELL HOLMES

One of the joys of being on *Sesame Street* is working with the wonderful people who write it, manage it, and perform on the program. In the thirty-four years since we began, we've lost a number of special people. One of them was Will Lee, who played Mr. Hooper.

Mr. Hooper was the show's grandfather figure. He gave gentle guidance to Big Bird when he'd go to Hooper's Store for birdseed milk shakes and advice.

Early in the show I came up with a joke I've used for years and years: I decided that Big Bird wouldn't be able to remember Mr. Hooper's name correctly. "Good morning, Mr. Looper!" greeted the Bird.

"Hooper! Hooper! My name is Hooper!" retorted Mr. Hooper.

The next time it would be "Tooper" or "Scooper" or even

"Mr. Pooper." One day I thought of a new one. "Good morning, Mr. Cunningham! Oh, gee, I wasn't even close!" I broke everyone up with that one.

Will Lee was one of the original Gang of Four—what we called the adult humans on the show. When he was booked on the program in 1969, he hadn't worked on television before. He'd been a stage actor in New York theater since the thirties but had gone through a long period when he couldn't get work. His name was on Senator McCarthy's blacklist of actors who were deemed a threat to national security—a huge injustice. He was a fine gentleman and actor, and I considered it a privilege to work with him.

During the twelfth season of *Sesame Street,* we could tell Will's health was suffering. He never mentioned it or complained. He occasionally missed a day of work, and one day he came into the studio not looking well at all. It was obvious he was very ill.

While we were standing around waiting for the set to be ready, I sat on the wall with him in front of Gordon's house. I was wearing the Bird's legs but not the puppet. I put my arm around his shoulder and said in the Bird's voice, "I love you, Mr. Looper."

He looked at me and said, "And I love you, Caroll." He went home soon after that, and I never saw him again. He died three days later of prostate cancer.

We were devastated by our loss, and we wondered how to deal with his passing on the show. It was argued that, since our

audience is so young, perhaps our story line should have him retire to Florida, to avoid dealing with the subject of death. Instead, it was decided that the show should be honest, and teach children something about loss.

A beautiful, sensitive script was written by our head writer at the time, Norman Stiles. In the story, Big Bird, who wants to be an artist, draws pictures of all the grown-ups on the show. He gives them out to Luis, Maria, Bob, Susan, and Gordon. "Where's Mr. Looper?" he asks. "I want to give him his picture."

Maria gently says, "Big Bird, don't you remember? We told you—Mr. Hooper died."

Big Bird replies, "I remember. Well, I'll give it to him when he comes back."

The grown-ups explain that when someone dies, they don't come back.

"He's not coming back—ever? But, but—that's so sad!" Big Bird cries.

When the scene ended, all the actors in the cast had genuine tears in their eyes. We used the first take, because it was so real. I think this scene was the best one we did in all the thirty-four years of *Sesame Street.* It was our tribute to Will Lee.

21

DON'T LET YOUR FEATHERS
GET RUFFLED

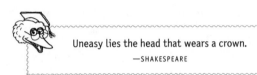

Uneasy lies the head that wears a crown.
—SHAKESPEARE

For the first fifteen years of *Sesame Street,* Big Bird was the surrogate child of the show. Like the first-born kid in any family, he enjoyed the attention and adoration of the grown-ups around him and the audience at home. It was wonderful for me as a performer. Many of the street stories centered on Big Bird. He was featured in the network specials, and *Sesame's* first feature film was *Follow That Bird.* As the major puppet on the street, Big Bird was in some ways the star of the show.

Then came Elmo.

Actually, the little red puppet has been around for quite a while. He debuted in one of the first seasons as Baby Monster. When the writers stopped writing scenes around the Monster Family, Baby Monster went into a storage drawer and waited there for his next script.

In the late seventies, a writer came up with an idea for a

new character called Elmo. No puppet was specified for the role, so Caroly Wilcox pulled the little red guy out of his drawer and sent him over to the studio. Brian Meehl was assigned the character. His interpretation of Elmo was a little different from the character we know today. He spoke with a whispery man's voice, and repeated words and phrases a lot. He sounded like this: "Play, play with Elmo? Yes? Yes?" When Brian left us to pursue other things, Elmo went back in the drawer.

A couple of years later, Elmo showed up in a script again. A young puppeteer named Kevin Clash got the part, put the puppet on his hand, and the character transformed into the Elmo we all know and love. Adorable, small, physical, and *very* positive (that laugh!), Elmo was a hit from the moment Kevin adopted the character.

Sesame Street's audience has gotten steadily younger since the show began. By playing Elmo as an energetic three-and-a-half-year-old, Kevin gives the younger crowd someone they can relate to perfectly. He moves the puppet wonderfully and is funny and expressive, giving Elmo a wide emotional range. And let's face it—Elmo is unbelievably cute. As soon as Kevin started playing Elmo, the audience loved him, and so did the producers and writers. He was on the A list of characters almost immediately and got a lot of attention.

For Big Bird, and for me, it was like having a new, younger brother in the family. It must have been what it was like for my brothers living with me when I became a show-off. Elmo was now the cute young child on the street. Big Bird became a little older, a little more self-reliant and mature. As time went on, Elmo started getting the top billing that Big Bird had had. Specials, products, and movies became Elmo driven, rather than Big Bird driven. The Bird was still in almost every episode of the show, but there was a new kid in town. I had to get used to sharing the attention, both in terms of my characters, and myself.

Big Bird has certainly not been forgotten. He remains popular with children and continues to be recognized and honored with awards. The *Sesame* producers and writers have created new segments for him on the show, and every episode begins with the Bird greeting the audience.

Sesame Street, I've come to realize, is a big place. It is almost unheard of to be on television for as long as we have, and to be known in as many countries and by as many people as we are. Sure, some characters become more popular than others for periods of time, but the show has always been a group effort in the service of our mission. Sharing and cooperation, getting along with others, and recognizing one another's strengths are some of our most important social messages, after all. I think there is enough room on *Sesame Street* for everyone.

22

FIND COMPASSION

We have to find a great deal more
kindness than is ever spoken.
—RALPH WALDO EMERSON

One evening in early December I had just finished a satisfying day of taping Big Bird's adventures. Instead of riding my bicycle home as usual, I decided to walk to my apartment. It was less than a mile from the old studio, straight down Broadway, and I was in fine spirits as I strolled. Snow was falling lightly, which helped put me in the mood for the coming Christmas season. At around Seventy-eighth Street I came upon an elderly man shuffling his feet at the edge of the sidewalk, taking tiny steps but not moving past the curb.

I glanced at him and thought perhaps he was another of the poor souls one often sees on Broadway—angry, disturbed, or simply drunk. I moved quickly past him without making eye contact and crossed the side street. Something made me look back at him. He was still in the same place, looking bewildered and upset. Maybe he wasn't drunk.

I went back to him and asked if he was all right. He said that he was afraid of falling on the wet pavement, and that he lived alone, so that if he hurt himself no one would look after him. I was mortified. All he wanted was a little help.

I took his arm, and we stepped down into the street. The thought came to me that this small step would seem huge and perilous if one was frail. I walked him several blocks to his door. He thanked me, and as I continued on home, I felt terrible that my first thought hadn't been compassion for this man. Then it hit me—if compassion is something lacking in the world, perhaps it's something we should teach on *Sesame Street*. Big Bird could do that. He could teach children about being compassionate.

The very next day I spoke to a producer about my idea.

"It's a nice thought, but how do you do that?" she asked. "How do you write compassion into the scripts?"

I had to admit that I couldn't immediately suggest a simple answer. I resolved to find ways to express compassion as part of Big Bird's nature, in the things he said and did, and the way he would deal with other characters on the show.

A couple of years later, in a newspaper article on

Sesame Street, a journalist profiling the various characters wrote: "... and then, there's the compassionate Big Bird." I knew that somehow I had done it, and compassion had come through Big Bird's character. That was one of the greatest compliments I have ever gotten for my work. If that journalist saw Big Bird's compassion, then the kids watching would likely see it too. I would really be doing something right, perhaps even important, if I was bringing even a little more compassion into the world through Big Bird.

23

BE GOOD TO EACH OTHER

 Friendship consists in forgetting what one gives and remembering what one receives.
—ALEXANDRE DUMAS

On May 16, 1990, at six forty-five in the morning, my phone rang. It was Anne Kinney, Jim Henson's personal secretary. She told me that she had some very sad news. Jim had fallen ill and had died early that morning. I couldn't believe my ears. How could Jim, one of the most vital individuals I'd ever known, be dead? "He died?" I stammered into the phone. "How could he die?"

Debra, who could only hear my side of the conversation, assumed that the news was that my eighty-nine-year-old father had passed away. She tried to console me.

"No, not Dad," I told her. "It's Jim!"

"Jim who?"

"Jim Henson!"

We both collapsed in anguish. It seemed the world that he

had built and included us in was gone in an instant. It was the end of Camelot.

When I first met Jim, I was somewhat in awe of him. The live shows I'd seen him put on—the ideas, the puppets, and the performances—were incredible. But the reason that his was the puppet troupe I most wanted to join was television. Since I had first seen it, I knew that puppets and television were a natural fit. When I saw Jim's commercials and TV appearances, I realized just how well puppets and television could be done.

I had been aware of Jim's work since 1960, when I first saw his Wilkin's coffee ads on television. He had two puppets against a simple backdrop. One puppet pointed a cannon at the other and asked, "Do you drink Wilkin's coffee?" The other puppet said, "No." The first puppet blew him away with his cannon and then pointed it at the camera and said, "Do you drink Wilkin's coffee?" That was the whole ad. It was brilliant—funny, sharp, and simple.

As inspiring as I found his work, I never thought to pursue working for Jim. Perhaps I was a bit intimidated, or maybe it was just that he was based in New York, which seemed so far away from my New England home. Whatever it was, I procrastinated and never went to him for a job. When he approached me about *Sesame Street,* though, I knew that "this was it!" *Sesame Street* had all the elements I wanted for my career: puppets, children's television, and Jim Henson.

After Jim hired me, I had to find an apartment in New York. I managed to get something close to the studio that I could afford, but I couldn't move in for a period of weeks. Jim invited me to stay a week in his home in Greenwich, Connecticut. I, of course, was delighted. I had the chance to get to know his family and enjoy lovely evenings of conversation. I played with his boys, Brian and John Paul. As I look back, it's amusing to think of Brian, who would one day become my boss, bouncing on my knees playing "Tony the Pony."

The next week I slept on a couch in Jim's office. For entertainment, he allowed me to watch his home movies. I think I'm one of the few people who ever saw him without his beard.

One of the wonderful aspects of Jim's genius was his openness to new ideas from the people around him. From the beginning, on our rides to and from New York, we'd talk about the possibilities of the new show. To my delight, Jim used several of my suggestions, like having a child sit with one of the puppets in an unscripted bit, talking about letters or numbers.

Jim was the hardest-working man I have ever met. He always had a number of things going at once, yet no matter how busy he was, he was also planning new things. He was like a juggler who could keep twenty things in the air at the same time.

All this he did with only a few hours of sleep a night. The

day he hired me he asked me how I liked to work. I didn't know what he meant, so he explained, "When I work with Frank Oz, we'll get into a project and work all day, all night, all the next day and sometimes all the next night too. Do you like to work like that?"

I should have been diplomatic and said that I did, but the truth will out. "No way!" I said. I like a solid eight hours' sleep every night. Jim could get by on an hour or two. Once in London, we left a party with him at 2:00 A.M. I was concerned about a nine o'clock call time that morning. Jim said that he'd be ready for it because he had a 5:00 A.M. meeting with Robert Altman first. He loved what he did so much, I don't think he thought of it as work. It was the way he lived.

One of Jim's greatest talents was the ability to gather talented people around him. He could always find the right people to do all the things he needed done. He liked people he could identify with, and hired people almost on instinct. Each person had his own particular talents, but Jim seemed as interested in the people themselves as in what they could bring to the organization.

I think another reason why Jim was so productive and successful was that he truly loved to collaborate. He had tremendous confidence in his ideas and in his builders, designers, and performers. He never micromanaged, and he never hovered, preferring to get something started and then let it grow. Jim loved to watch an idea take on a life of its own, with contributions from everyone involved. He gave his people free rein and more often than not was happily surprised with the results.

I never saw Jim get angry. If he was upset, he would move away from people and appear to brood. He never raised his voice with anyone who worked for him. He didn't have to motivate people that way. As a performer working for Jim, you believed in his genius and wanted to be a part of it. I wanted to do my best for him all the time, and when I couldn't give him what I knew he wanted, I felt frustrated and impotent, like when he imagined the elaborate dance for Big Bird on *The Muppet Show*. After that disaster, I told him that I thought Big Bird's talents lay in other directions and that if he had me on again, I hoped that he'd let me do what I was good at. Jim listened. In the *Muppet Family Christmas* special, he created a delightful scene with Big Bird and the Swedish Chef that played to my strengths as a performer and Big Bird's as a character.

While Jim wouldn't say anything negative about a performer or a performance, he also wasn't one to gush with high praise. If something was to his liking, he would say, "Mmmm." If he really liked it, he might softly say, "Lovely." I think Jim felt that the thing we were working on should speak for itself, and he'd rather save his energy for thinking up new projects than complimenting the ones that were done.

In the second season of *Sesame Street,* I had a neat experience. Production had become so busy that while street scenes were being taped at the main studio, other Muppet scenes were being taped at a studio at ABC. I was the only puppeteer on the main set and didn't see the other puppeteers much at all. One day, while I was leaving, Jim was coming in. "Ah, Muppets West," he said. From Jim, this was a huge compliment. He meant that he considered me to be his representative at the studio. I told him that I was flattered. He said, "I mean that. You've really been carrying it wonderfully. Thank you." Hearing that from Jim was extremely satisfying. I felt like he was saying that he hadn't made a mistake when he picked me to play the Bird and Oscar.

I was doing Ernie's right hand with Jim one day, and after the scene was done, Jim dropped the puppet on the floor. He had to get a prop, and since Ernie was in his way, he nudged him aside with his foot. I picked Ernie up and said to him, "Oh, Ernie. Jim didn't mean to do that."

Jim said, "Yes, I did. He was in my way." Then he asked, "Do you really talk to the puppets?"

I told him that I did. When I drop Picklepuss, I apologize to him.

Jim smiled. He said, "To me, the puppets are just tools to get the scenes done. I'm not sentimental about them."

Business suits were not for Jim. He'd wear "cool" clothes, peasant shirts and one-of-a-kind items he'd find in his travels. Amusingly, in the early years, his trousers were always much too short, exposing four inches of his ankles, which rather spoiled the overall appearance of his outfit. Still, he had such charisma that he virtually glowed, almost as if he were lit from inside.

When Jim first hired me, he was thirty-two and I was thirty-five. I think he saw some of himself in me. He told me that as a kid he'd wanted something of the good life. Like me, he wanted things that he saw but couldn't have, and he decided that one day he'd get them. We became pals. He'd call up when he needed a break and we'd go see a movie. Or we'd get together for the evening and talk. Any time Deb and I got to spend with him was quality time, whether it was going to dinner or attending one of his beautiful and expensive parties or masquerade balls. He loved tuxedo nights and limousines, and it was thrilling to be included in an evening with Jim.

Life around Jim was fun. On the set he was mischievous and hilarious. He had an impish side, and when it showed, you could see where Ernie's character came from. When Jim worked with Frank Oz, he treated him pretty much the way

Ernie treats Bert. In rehearsals, or while waiting for the cameras and lights to be ready, Jim would tease Frank by having Ernie send up Bert. His jokes would be on the mark but never unkind. Jim and Frank were very close, and their working relationship was the essence of what the Muppets were all about.

Jim knew how to enjoy life when he wasn't working too. In 1960, before he was really successful, he drove a Rolls-Royce. In the late seventies, when he was living in London, he ordered a Lotus Elite and had it painted Kermit the Frog green. It had round, pop-up headlights with Kermit eyes painted on them. The day he went to take delivery, it was stolen. The thieves used it as a get-away car that afternoon. They were caught right away, and the car was unharmed. When I visited Jim in London, he'd drive me around in the Lotus, going sixty miles an hour between traffic lights. Eventually, he bought a Volkswagen Rabbit convertible, the only car he could keep without it being stolen.

Nobody threw parties like Jim did. He spent over one hundred thousand dollars on a party at the Waldorf. Half of the cost was for the decoration. He turned the room into a bayou, with real Spanish moss hanging down from crookedy trees, and I bumped into people like Linda Gray and Bernadette Peters. Another time, Jim flew everyone who worked for him to Bermuda for a weekend conference. All of the people who knew Jim loved to go to his lavish parties.

Some years before it happened, Jim left instructions for what to do in case he died. He said that there shouldn't be a funeral. If people wanted to remember him, it should be at a celebration. No one should wear black; celebrants should be dressed in bright and jolly colors. He wanted there to be puppets, and singing, and happy stories told. When Jim died, the celebration was held at the Cathedral of St. John the Divine. It was open to anyone who wanted to come, and thousands did. Brian Henson asked me to come as Big Bird and sing "It's Not Easy Being Green," which has always been Kermit's signature song. Somehow I managed to do it without crying. People held up hundreds of butterfly puppets that had been made for the event, and all the major Muppets were in attendance. Jim had written letters to his five children to be opened only after his death. Brian read from his. Jim wrote, "Be good to each other. Love and forgive everybody." I remembered Jim telling me that he never wasted energy on hating anybody; he had too much thinking to do.

The celebration ended as Jim had planned. The Christian Temperance Society Band from New Orleans played "When the Saints Go Marching In," and we all marched out of the cathedral, crying, singing, and smiling.

24

GIVE SOMETHING BACK

> A good imitation is
> the most perfect originality.
> —WERNHER VON BRAUN

n 1997, after years of negotiations, China finally got a *Sesame Street* of its own.

There are more than twenty international versions of *Sesame Street* all over the world. These are independent productions, not the U.S. version of the show in translation. When they first thought about bringing *Sesame* to other countries, they realized that to really give children the kind of messages they needed most, the show would have to be done locally, with local talent, educational advisors, and producers.

These shows are based on *Sesame Street* but have different sets, characters, and themes. The one in Norway takes place entirely outdoors, for example, and there even is a *Sesame Street* being produced by Israelis, Palestinians, and Jordanians together. Many of them have a big puppet—Russia has a big blue ghost based on a character from folklore; Mexico has a

parrot; Brazil had an alligator—but nobody else was allowed to have Big Bird.

When the Chinese were working on developing their show, they insisted that they should have Big Bird. He was still quite popular in China because of *Big Bird in China,* and they wouldn't do the show without him. CTW finally agreed, and I was sent back to China again, this time to cast and train Da Niao, the Chinese Big Bird.

Kevin Clash, in addition to playing Elmo, is also the Muppets' puppet director. An excellent instructor, he was in charge of auditions and training for *Zhima Jie,* which is what the Chinese called their show. When I arrived in Shanghai, he had found four candidates to play Da Niao. It was up to me to decide which fellow would become my Chinese counterpart, and I was very excited. I loved the idea of there being a Big

Bird on the other side of the world, and I was happy to give China its own Big Bird after China had given me so much.

The tryouts of would-be puppeteers took place in a school building. Kevin had started with more than a hundred applicants, and he had chosen the best four to audition for me.

I was able to eliminate one fellow after watching him perform for just a few minutes. He had been heavily trained in traditional Chinese puppetry, which is a beautiful, formal style. When he put on the Bird, he instinctively began to go through the poses that Chinese characters use for expression. This style of movement just doesn't work for Big Bird and doesn't fit the rules that Jim Henson established for the Muppets years ago. He also was afraid of walking in the costume. This is understandable, because it's claustrophobic in there, with no way to actually see out and only the tiny television monitor as your guide. He walked around as if he were walking on the edge of the roof of a very tall building while wearing a blindfold.

The second fellow didn't have any acting ability, so it was quickly down to two. I was torn. Both were excellent at moving the Bird. They were also both very nice people, and friends besides. One liked to be called Jack. He was good, but I was told that he had a strong Shanghai street accent—sort of like having a Brooklyn accent in the States. It would typecast him and also make it hard for people in many parts of China to understand him. His competitor, Mien Mien, had a more neutral accent and would sound better to people all over China. It also helped that he was unusually tall for a Chinese person. He was taller than me, about six feet, and slender. But what really made up my mind was that he had the most gentle and thoughtful personality, which is important for playing Big Bird—especially, I thought, in China, where the only things for children to watch on TV were Japanese cartoons, which tend to be aggressive, violent, and not particularly educational. The producers of *Zhima Jie* wanted compassion to be one of the main themes for the first season. They felt that Chinese kids could really benefit from watching characters being kind and caring toward one another, and I wanted that for their Big Bird. Mien Mien impressed me as being compassionate, sweet, and thoughtful.

I chose Mien Mien, and Jack took it well. The first two fellows that I had already cut cried when they were turned down; now Mien Mien cried when he got the part. He said that it was his father's fiftieth birthday and it would make him proud. I drew a picture of Mien Mien playing Da Niao as a present for his dad.

When I picked Mien Mien to play Big Bird, I thought about what it was like when Jim picked me and how much my life had changed since that moment. My career, meeting Debra, and of course visiting China had all come about from Jim's invitation to play the Bird. Whatever Mien Mien had before him, I hoped it would be as wonderful for him as it had been for me. I also thought about how curious it was that Big Bird had taken me to China and now I had given China its own Da Niao. I taught Mien Mien all I could in the short time I had.

The Chinese *Sesame Street* came together very well. The characters, a blue furry Muppet pig, a red and furry little-girl monster who looked a lot like *Sesame Street's* Zoe, and Da Niao taught lessons about relationships and social themes. The show was well liked, but sadly, the Chinese government stopped financing it, and production has ceased. I think the money would have been well invested, if only they had helped the program to grow. It was the first attempt made to create educational television material for the millions of children who normally only get to see cartoons that use violence to solve their story situations. China needs *Sesame Street* or something a lot like it.

Still, it's a wonderful feeling to know that, at least for a while, Da Niao danced and sang along with the children in China, while I played Big Bird on the other side of the world.

25

FIND YOUR PLACE IN THE WORLD

Fame is a thin shadow of eternity.
—THOMAS FULLER

I may be the most unknown famous person in America.

It's the Bird who's famous, not me. Most actors and performers who are as well known as Big Bird get invited to big parties and are hounded by the press. Me, I can walk down the street and nobody knows who I am, unless I want them to. For a long time I avoided personal publicity because I had no interest in fame. After all, if you become famous, you have to become accustomed to having strangers walk up to you and talk to you—they know you, but you don't know them. I love to perform, but I also love my private life.

Some good puppeteers have left *Sesame Street* because they became frustrated with not being recognized. That's a disadvantage of working with puppets, if recognition is what you're after. To me, though, puppets give me the guts to do things I would never do if everyone were looking at me. If I'm in a puppet, I can be unlike myself and act like a Grouch or sing and dance in front of a huge audience. Puppets and costumes can free a performer from being self-conscious and let characters come out from inside. And it's my characters that people want to see, not me.

In 1990 the Television Hall of Fame named *Sesame Street* Best Children's Show. Joan Ganz Cooney, the creator of the show, and Big Bird were invited to attend the ceremony.

Debra and I arrived in a limousine, dressed in gown and tux. We were asked to walk down the red-carpet entrance, which was lined with photographers snapping pictures of the stars as they came along. When Deb and I walked in, all cameras went down. No one had any idea who we were. Deb smiled at the bunch and said, "You may not recognize this man, but he's Big Bird on *Sesame Street!*" One camera came up and snapped a picture.

Later Diane Sawyer handed Big Bird an award onstage. The audience broke into cheers and applause. Inside the Bird I smiled, and I had him wave and thank the crowd and Diane Sawyer. He was the famous one, the one winning the award. I'm a puppeteer. Big Bird is a star.

While people usually respond enthusiastically when they hear what I do, not everyone is impressed.

A couple of years ago I was at a newsstand when *Life* magazine caught my eye. It was an issue commemorating fifty years of television, and along with Lucille Ball, Bart Simpson, Milton Berle, Joan Collins, and the *60 Minutes* stopwatch, there was a beautiful picture of Big Bird on the cover.

"I'll be darned!" I said out loud. "It's not often that I get on the cover of *Life* magazine."

The woman behind the counter was skeptical. "What do you mean?"

I pointed to Big Bird and said, "I play him. I'm Big Bird."

She rolled her eyes and said, "Well, I wouldn't tell people about it."

I'm very proud to have won four Emmys and two Grammys for my work as Big Bird and Oscar. I'm also proud of Big Bird's star on the Hollywood Walk of Fame. These awards mean a lot to me, because they reflect a certain level of achievement as an entertainer and a performer. I'm happy that the industry I've spent my life working in considers my work and my characters to be worthy of these honors.

But there's another award that I received that makes me even more proud. This one seems more important, because it says that Big Bird, beyond being part of television, is part of the fabric of our country and our culture.

On April 24, 2000, the Library of Congress celebrated its two-hundredth birthday by naming eighty-one Americans as recipients of the first—and so far only—Living Legend Award. The award was established to honor individuals "who have made a significant contribution to America's cultural, scientific and social heritage." Among the honorees are Tiger Woods, Bob Hope, Jeane Kirkpatrick, I. M. Pei, Hank Aaron, Gloria Steinem, Isaac Stern—and Big Bird.

The Living Legends were gathered together for a televised medal presentation on the Capitol grounds. I was the only one who couldn't see what was going on, because I was in the Bird and could only peek out through a space between feathers. Big Bird presented the Library with a birthday cake, and I led the singing of "Happy Birthday."

Shortly after the ceremony, we were all invited to the Members Room of the Library for a reception. I was amazed

by some of the faces that were there—athletes, scientists, statesmen. I struck up a conversation with historian Jaroslav Pelikan, a scholar from Yale. He joked that his last name put him in the same class as Big Bird. I asked him if he was going to wear his medal, and he answered, "You bet! This is the only day you could wear it and not have people think you're crazy." The medal is a huge bronze disc hanging on a red, white, and blue ribbon. I keep mine in its box, which reads: LIVING LEGEND—CAROLL SPINNEY (BIG BIRD).

Later that day when I got on the air shuttle to New York, there were five people on the plane wearing their medals. One of them was Colin Powell, who saw an empty seat next to Deb and me and joked, "Ah, I see you've saved me a seat!"

I had always hoped to have one of my characters become a show-business success. I never dreamed that playing Big Bird would allow me to be honored as a national treasure. Big Bird's fame is a funny thing, because he's a fantasy figure. In a way, he's not even real. Yet he lives and is famous. I have a little fame but an absolutely wonderful life. I like it that way.

26

REMEMBER THE FUTURE

The future influences the
present as much as the past.
—FRIEDRICH WILHELM NIETZSCHE

ig Bird is something that I always knew I'd be.

I couldn't have named him, of course, but I knew that I would be doing puppets on television, on the best children's show on television. I said so when I was twelve, and I was absolutely positive that I would do it.

At the World's Fair in 1940 I saw television for the first time. A woman was standing there singing, and she was also singing on a tiny twelve-inch screen next to her. That didn't make too deep an impression on me, but a television in a comic strip did. In *Nancy and Sluggo,* Fritzy Ritz had a huge console television in her living room. I remember looking at it and thinking—the idea just came to me—a television looks a lot like a puppet theater. I wanted to do puppets on television. I hadn't even seen it done, but I knew that it could be.

In 1947, when television first reached the Boston area, our family doctor, Dr. Forbes, would invite the neighborhood children to his house to watch a kids' show at five o'clock on WBZ-TV Boston. I rode my bike down there, quite a long way for me at the time, to see the show and was delighted to see that it included a character who was a puppet. I was even more delighted when I saw how bad it was. There was a man with an oven mitt on his hand, which was supposedly a swan, and he was terrible. I was twelve years old, and I knew that I already did better puppet shows. It gave me a tremendous boost of confidence. I said, "If he's on television, and getting *paid* for it, then when I grow up I'll do puppets on TV, and I'll do a lot better than that guy!"

It didn't just happen. I didn't expect to just win the lottery. I knew I'd get a show, but I had to do everything I could to expose myself. Someone once said, "The harder you work, the more luck you'll get," and I've found that to be true. I always felt that if somebody like Jim met me, he would see that I was what he needed for what he was doing.

The *Bozo* show paid well, but it got so that I hardly had to work. It wasn't the thing I had dreamed of as a boy. I wanted more, to educate, to do something artful, meaningful. When Jim offered me Big Bird, I knew that was it.

Every day on *Sesame Street*, we strive to give our innocent young audience the basis of a lifelong education. We teach some of the fundamentals of reading and numbers, but more important, we try to encourage children to develop the attitudes they need to live happy and productive lives: self-confidence, persistence, imagination, tolerance, compassion, curiosity, openness, respect, humor, and love, to name a few. It is no accident that spending the past thirty-four years in the Bird suit teaching these things to others has taught me a few things, too.

One of the simplest and most wonderful things I've learned is to love my job. The modus operandi of the show is humor, and the fun and laughter of the scripts spill over into the work atmosphere, making almost every day of work a pleasure, rather than a labor. The children watching the show will not learn anything from us if they are not first engaged by what they see, which requires the performers to be as charming, empathetic, honest,

and funny as we can be. We have to keep the kids watching
and listening through the appeal of our characters so that our
real points can be made. The puppets are our tools and alter
egos, and we are actors who do the acting at the ends of our
arms. Every script is a new challenge with the same goal: to
give something important to the audience, to the children. It
is easy to find the inspiration to do the work I'm paid to do.

The most important lesson I've learned is that first you
have to dream, and then you have to believe in your dreams.
That is the only way for them to come true. There will be set-
backs and disappointments, but do not let them deter you
from your plans, your beliefs, your dreams. Dare to dream. If
you don't, your dreams will never come to be. Imagine your
world the way you want it to be, then try to make it that way.
That's what Big Bird teaches on *Sesame Street*, and that's what
I've learned from playing him. Dream on.

There is something strange that happens to me every once
in a while: I remember the future. I think it's my way of
making my dreams come true. I vividly remember things happening before they do. Years ago, I remember walking into a
television show and performing characters long before I ever
did it.

Sometimes, when I'm at work and I've got my scripts in my
hand, and I'm clomping along in my big, funny feet, I chuckle

to myself in delight. I think I have the best job in the world. People ask me, "Are you surprised with the way your life has turned out?" No. I'm not surprised at all. I always believed that I would be doing this. And I'm so glad that I am.

ACKNOWLEDGMENTS

Caroll and J thank: our agent, Christy Fletcher, for taking us on and making this book happen; Whitney Lee, Liza Bolitzer, and everyone at Carlisle, for their enthusiasm and professionalism; our editor, Jon Karp, for his vision, intelligence, and ruthless cuts; Janelle Duryea, Jake Greenberg, Jonathan Jao, Casey Hampton, Daniel Rembert, Todd Doughty, and everyone at Random House, for making it easy; and La Fenice for the risotto.

Caroll thanks: my wife, Debra, for helping me remember lots of the details of this book, and everything else she does every day; Jim and Jane Henson, for creating a world and inviting me inside; Joan Ganz Cooney and all my great friends at *Sesame Street;* and J Milligan, who now knows me like a book—I couldn't have done it without you. I'd also like to thank the Academy . . . oops, wrong speech!

J thanks: my wife, Amy Yang, for her drive, ideas, and snap-out-of-it slaps; Miles Ludwig and Jack McCall, for the little push that started everything; Sabin Streeter, for publishing me first, and for all his help; Laurent Linn, Michael Schupbach, and Judy Freudberg, for helping me get inside the Bird; my family and friends, for letting me believe in all possibilities; and, of course, Caroll and Debra Spinney, who said yes, who trusted me to help Caroll share his wisdom with the world, and who let Wednesday visit anytime. Thank you.

For more information on The Puppeteers of America, write to:

The Puppeteers of America
Membership Office
P.O. Box 29417
Parma, OH 44129-0417

ABOUT THE AUTHOR

Caroll Spinney has performed as Big Bird and Oscar on *Sesame Street* since the show's inception in 1969. Prior to that, he performed as many characters on *Bozo's Big Top* in Boston for ten years, had a career in art and animation, and served in the Air Force. He has traveled the world as Big Bird, won Grammys and Emmys, and been named a Living Legend by the Library of Congress. He lives in New England with his wife, Debra. They have three children and three grandchildren.

ABOUT THE WRITER

J MILLIGAN was the creative director and head writer at Sesame Workshop's interactive department for five years. In addition to writing for the *Sesame Street* characters and designing games, Milligan has had work published in *The New Yorker* and *XXL* magazine and on word.com. He has completed his first novel, *Jack Fish,* and consults for Sesame Workshop on projects in various media. He lives in Brooklyn with his wife, the artist Amy Yang. They have three cats and a dog.